Royal Tunbridge Wells
in old picture postcards

by Margaret A.V. Gill

European Library ZALTBOMMEL / THE NETHERLANDS

Cover picture:

Postcard published circa 1924.

BACK IN TIME

GB ISBN 90 288 2564 9

Second edition, 1999: reprint of the original edition of 1983.

INTRODUCTION

If you were suddenly to find yourself in Tunbridge Wells without knowing anything about it, you would at once perceive that it was a place with history wrote an American visitor to Tunbridge Wells in 1908. Histories and guide books of the town abound, so it is not the intention here either to relate the town's early history and development following the discovery of the chalybeate spring by Lord North in 1606 or to act as a guide for the modern tourist to its historic edifices, but rather to evoke the image of Tunbridge Wells of between fifty and a hundred years ago as described in contemporary literature, seen through the eyes of the photographer and recorded on early picture postcards. To some it may come as a surprise to discover how many changes have taken place during the last fifty years; old buildings have been demolished and new erected in their stead. More unexpected, however, has been the transformation in the appearance of the Common, which has always been an integral part of the town and its life.

On Tunbridge Wells Common, explained the author of a late Victorian guide, contrasting the spa with coastal watering-places, *there are no niggers (minstrels), no switchbacks, no bathing machines, and nobody wants them, but there are rocks – bold and impressive; there are 179 acres of soft springy sward that makes walking a delight; there is golden-tipped gorse in such profusion that no artist would or could dare to transfer its brilliant abundance to a canvas. There are walks and rambles, and nooks and corners, and avenues, and far-stretching views such as no country but Old England and no counties but Kent and Sussex can produce.* The supplanting of open heathland by young and maturing woodland has come about so gradually as to pass unnoticed by the majority of local inhabitants, but comparison of present vistas with the panoramas on Edwardian cards emphasises the extent of change.

The atmosphere of Edwardian Tunbridge Wells, despite the developments and innovations of the latter part of Victoria's reign, was much the same as induced the author William Gaspey earlier to summarise for the benefit of his readers the leading characteristics of the place in his

TRIBUTE TO TUNBRIDGE WELLS

Weary of town, where endless work
Saps of our strength the citadels,
Where evils in the system lurk, –
Let us away to Tunbridge Wells.

No place within our favoured isle
For rural beauty this excels;
No place more sweetly can beguile
Our leisure hours, than Tunbridge Wells.

Touching its worth in ancient days,
Fame many a lively legend tells,
And modern times unite to praise
The attributes of Tunbridge Wells.

The Walks, the Waters, the Parade,
Dear equally to beaux and belles,
Prove art and nature both have made
A Nonpareil *of Tunbridge Wells.*

Its climate, redolent of balm,
Depression from the breast expels,
And care-worn pilgrims, seeking calm,
Direct their steps to Tunbridge Wells:

Then, quaffing from the Springs which flow
With blessings from Earth's inmost cells,
They to their homes, rejoicing, go,
Strengthened, restored, by Tunbridge Wells.

Illustrations:
From the postcard collection of Tunbridge Wells Municipal Museum; except 67 (T.A. Griffiths).

Principal sources quoted:
Brackett: A Handy Book for Visitors to Tunbridge Wells (1880): 12, 46.
F. Field: Comic Guide to Tunbridge Wells (1880): 16.
Pictorial History of Tunbridge Wells (1892): 11, 88.
Pelton's Illustrated Guide to Tunbridge Wells (15th edition 1896): 2, 3, 5, 10, 20, 24, 48, 55, 86, 91.
W.S. Martin and B.P. Row: Tunbridge Wells of To-day (about 1897): 44, 87.
Official Town Guides (1902): 6, 63, (1908): 80, 81, (1909): 69, (1920s): 4, (1933): 65, (1935): 57, (1937): 66.
Kent and Sussex Courier (25-9-1896): 64, (9-4-1897): 64, (27-4-1906): 15, (21-6-1907): 58, (26-7-1907): 76, (3-1-1908): 58, (13-5-1910): 54, (23-6-1911): 38, (29-11-1912): 29, (25-4-1913): 52, (2-5-1913): 52, (31-7-1914): 17, (7-8-1914): 8, (18-9-1914): 55, 56, (25-7-1919): 31, (1-8-1919): 21, (26-5-1922): 30, 65, (9-1-1925): 85, (19-5-1939): 11, (27-2-1970): 7.
Tunbridge Wells Advertiser (24-9-1897): 60, (1-10-1897): 60, (8-9-1899): 68, (28-4-1905): 28, (17-5-1907): 28, (16-2-1923): 32.
C.H. Strange: The Jubilee of Tunbridge Wells as an Incorporated Borough: 1, 6.
Official Programme of Arrangements to Celebrate the Coronation of George V (1911): 26, 27, 37.
King Charles School Log Book: 18.
H.A. Waring: The Story of King Charles-the-Martyr (1937): 61.
F. Roberts: Pen and Ink Sketches, in the Guide to the High Rocks (undated): 92.
A. Savidge: Royal Tunbridge Wells (1975, quotation from Daily Telegraph 1879): 40.
J. King: Buses and Bathchairs... But not a Tram in Sight (1976): 72.

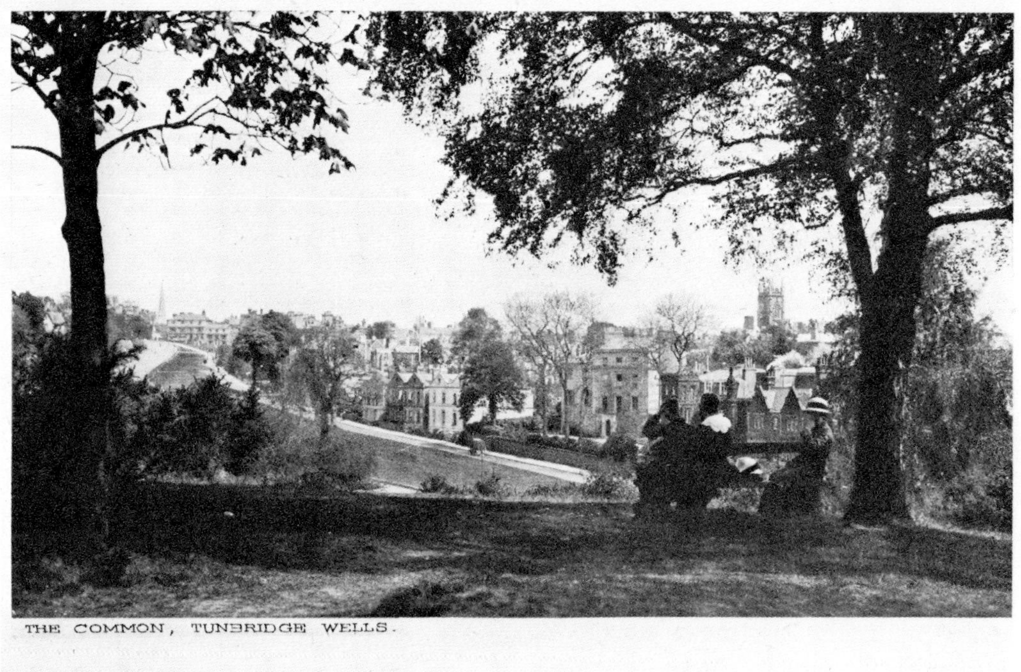

1. *A town of open spaces, a town of churches and chiming bells, a town of trees and lawns and flower gardens, a town of sunshine and sweet air and pure water, a town of culture and recreation and healing – a place to live in, a place to be ill and get well in, a place to die in* – so Charles Hilbert Strange concluded his Jubilee account of the Borough's history since its Incorporation in 1889. Those fifty years (more or less the period covered by this book) saw many changes in the topography of the town and in the way of life of its inhabitants. This Edwardian postcard, with the skyline still dominated by church tower and spire, epitomises the tranquility of the town when motor vehicles though not unknown were rare.

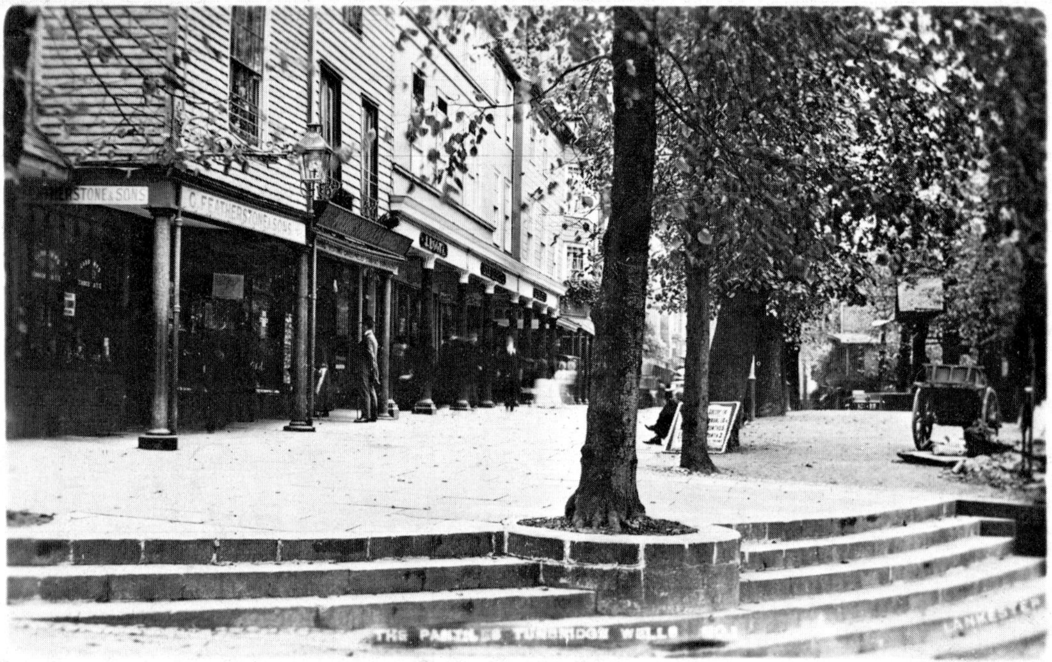

2. *The first place which... the visitor to Tunbridge Wells will wish to see, is the Pantiles, known to many under the older name of the 'Walks'. There is nothing exactly corresponding to this promenade in any other English watering-place; and the observation made by many a stranger upon the first sight of this unique parade, is, 'How antique, how un-English, how foreign!' It is indeed an old-world spot; and it is an advantage that some of the houses which have been more recently erected, in place of those which have decayed through age, have been built in the old-fashioned, gabled style, preserving in some degree the quaintness of its appearance, although others are not of a style that is worthy of such a situation... Until a comparatively recent period, there was a lower as well as an upper walk; an avenue of trees served to separate the one from the other, and to afford shade to both. But the lower walk has now been raised to the higher level.*

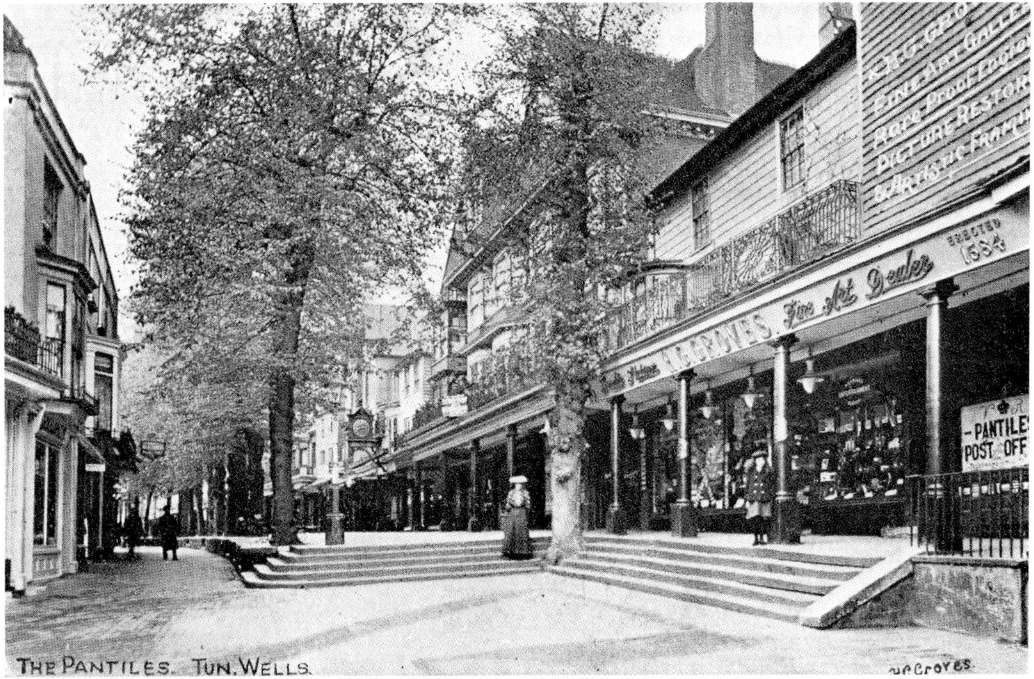

3. *This boulevard of Tunbridge Wells is... still a favourite lounge of the company, who, meeting here, some to drink the waters, and some to 'see and to be seen' promenade on the level pavement, sit beneath the shade of a pretty arcade of lime trees, or amuse themselves beneath the colonnade by inspecting the millinery, the jewellery, the photographs, the books, and other articles displayed for sale.* The Pantiles Post Office and Art Shop overlooking Bath Square feature prominently in this view published by H.G. Groves, who inserted additional advertisement on the weatherboarding in the photograph which was never inscribed there in reality. In 1915 the Post Office moved to new premises further along the Pantiles; in 1938 Nos. 30-36 (just beyond the clock) were demolished. The gap, now converted into a memorial garden, is the subject of much controversy as to whether or not new buildings should be constructed on the site.

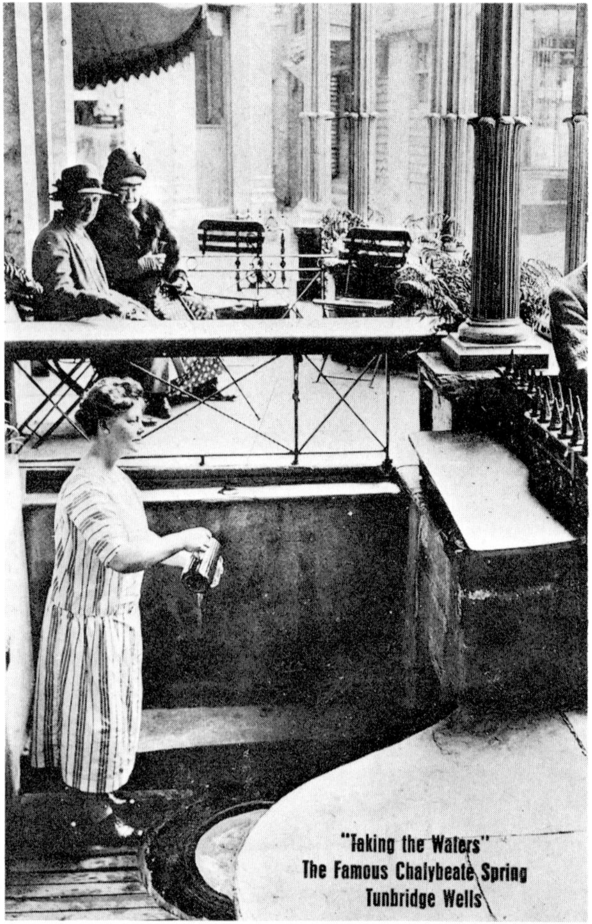

4. Nowadays no one seriously takes the waters at the Chalybeate Spring in Bath Square though a dipper is still in regular attendance during the tourist season to supply visitors with a sample glass. As late as the 1920's, however, the Official Guide extolled the water as 'a most potent tonic' and reiterated 'for the assurance of intending drinkers the report of an eminent Analyst'. According to this nineteenth century doctor, the water contained *iron altogether in the state of ferrous carbonate... the form which is most preferred where a mild and non-astringent chalybeate is desired as most easy of digestion and assimilation... a water of pleasing appearance, complete limpidity, absolute purity, and with entire absence of disagreeable styptic taste.* An earlier visitor expressed amusement at observing *the folks drink their glasses and then diligently scrub their teeth over with sage leaves to remove the marks of iron.*

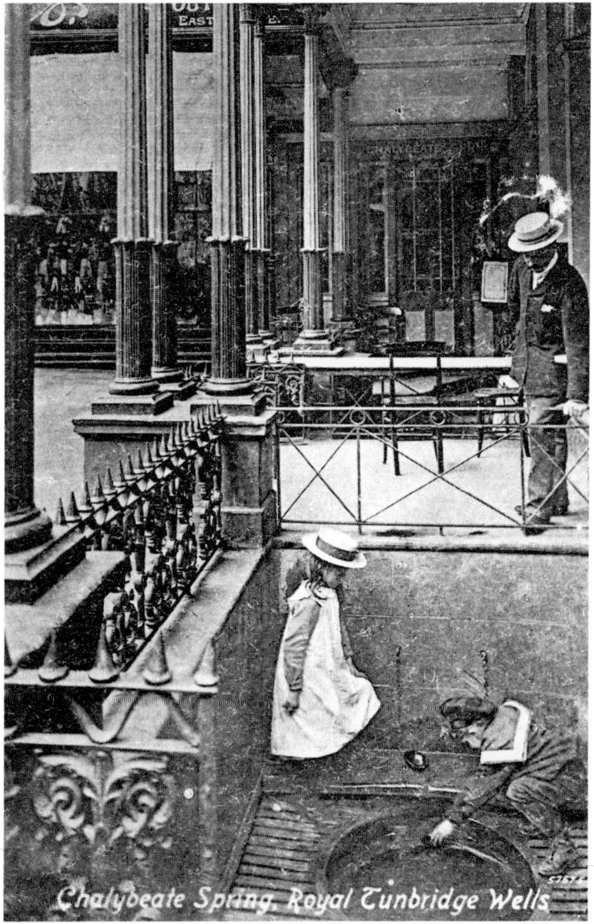

5. While from early days water was served by dippers for a small remuneration from the first of two stone basins, in accordance with a Parliamentary resolution of 1739/40 making the spring free to the public in perpetuity, the overflow gathered in the second basin remained open at all times and gratuitous. The present portico with its cast iron columns and railings was added to the neo-classical Bath House in 1847, at which time the old plunging bath connected with the spring was abolished, having already fallen into disuse. Since in summer the spring produced scarcely more than one gallon per minute, it took a long time to fill even one bath, and since the iron was quickly deposited once the water had left its source, bathers found themselves plunging into a 'stagnant, turbid, rusty pool' only to emerge 'in a condition very much resembling a hide from a tanner's yard'.

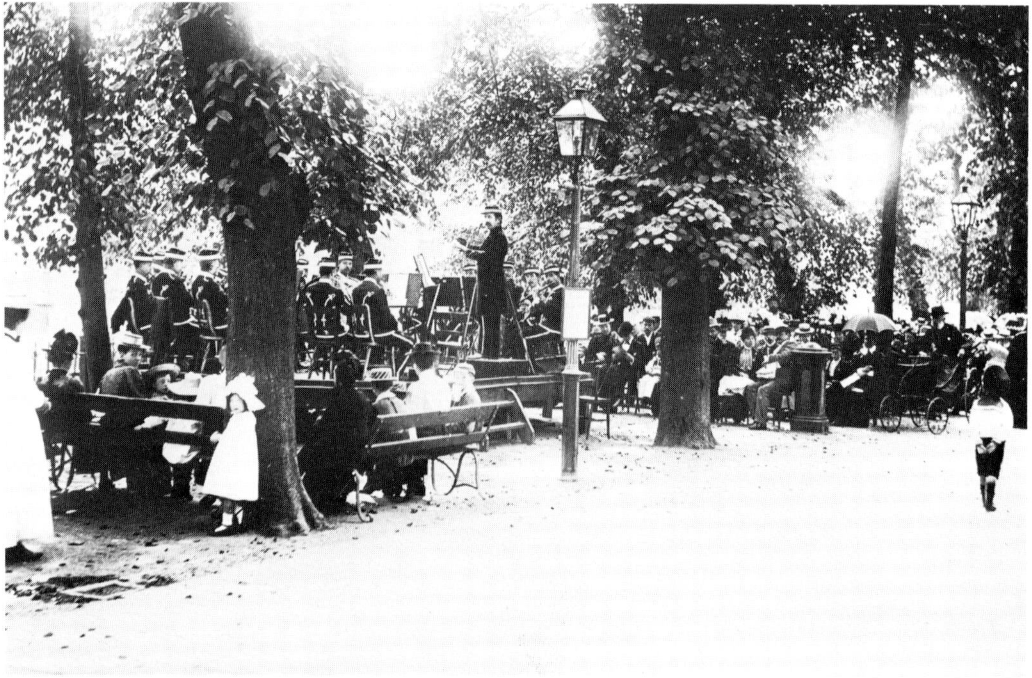

6. *In this charming spot, shaded by an avenue of limes, and bordered on one side by a row of quaint old shops, with a piazza running along its entire length, they foregather in the morning to enjoy the delight of gossip and badinage and the music of the Corporation Band;* thus wrote the first Official Guide. The Town Band in its scarlet and white uniforms playing wind instruments, was a familiar sight on the Pantiles, the Common and at street corners during the latter part of Victoria's reign and early years of this century. After accepting an engagement for a world cruise on S.S. Ceylon, it was known as the Ceylon Band. With time, the band dwindled till finally there was but one cornet player 'whose somewhat melancholy solos, in weather fair, foul or cold, only ceased when, poor man, he could no longer play'. He afterwards sat as a model for students at the Art School. The photograph of the Band on this card dates back to the 1890's.

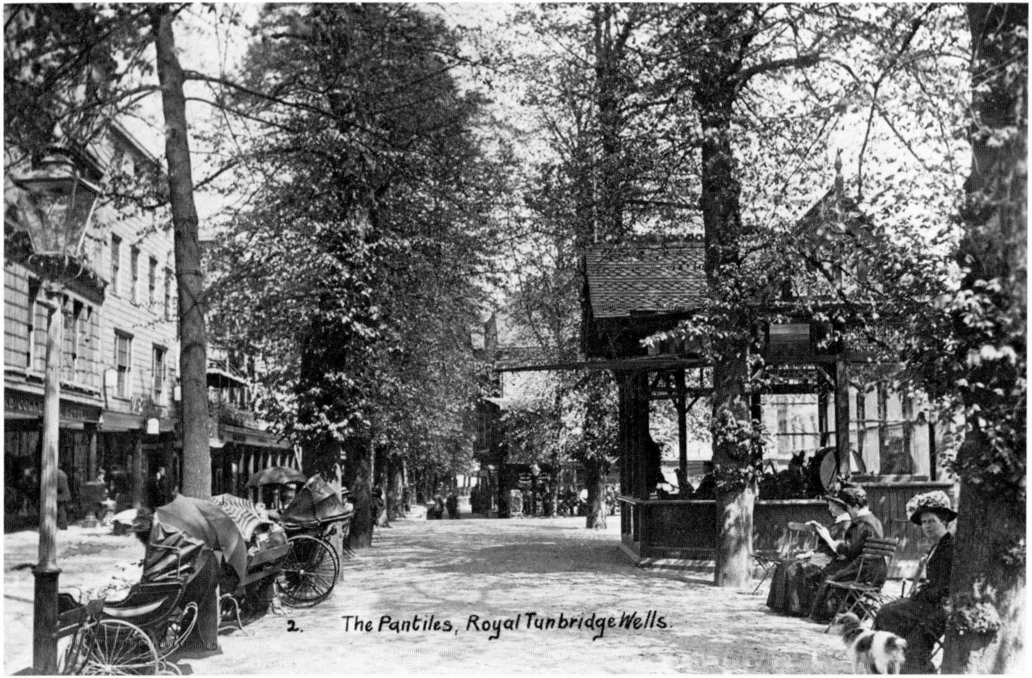

7. Although the old music gallery, described by Thackeray as 'a weak little old balcony' still existed at the end of the century, irreverently nicknamed 'The Dutch Oven', the Town Band played in the open on the Pantiles (see previous postcard). In 1900 the covered bandstand seen here was erected, opening on 13th September with a special concert. For the occasion the Borough Band was augmented by the London Professional Instrumentalists and The English Opera Singers, who included in the programme a quartet from Gilbert and Sullivan's 'Yeoman of the Guard' and 'On the Road to Mandalay'. By 1969 its condition was considered dangerous, *offers by local traders to raise money for its repair were refused, and it was demolished in plenty of time for the town council entertainments committee's son et lumiere production – to which it would have proved something of an embarrassment.* In May 1973 the present open-air stage was opened.

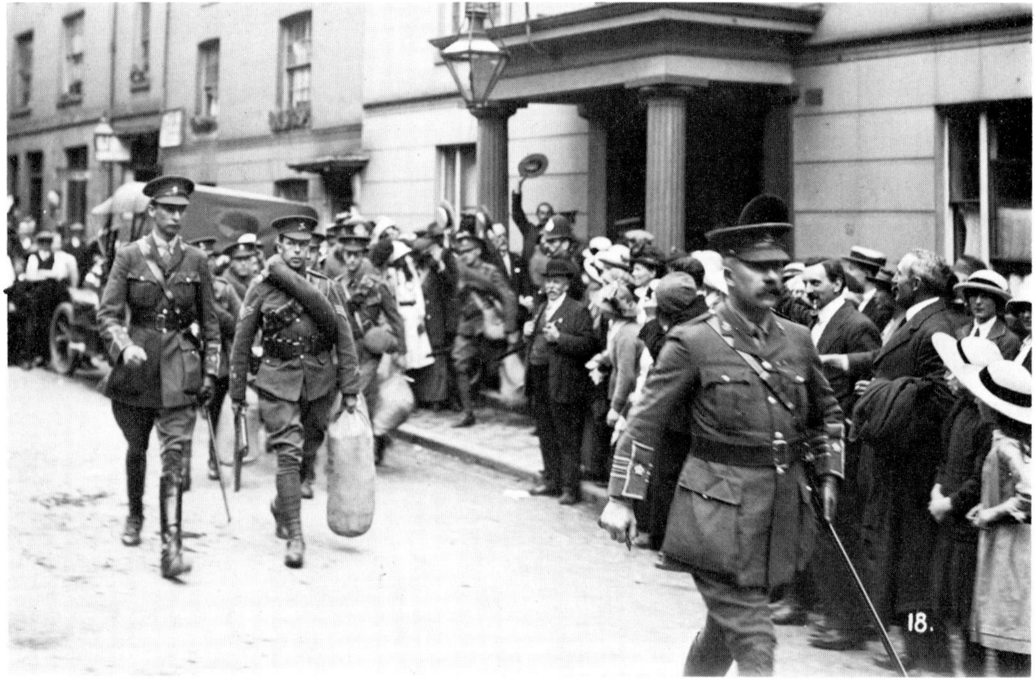

8. The C Squadron West Kent Yeomanry are seen here leaving the Corn Exchange which served as their drill hall. They had arrived back from camp at Aldershot on 4th August 1914 and almost immediately set out to join the other squadrons at Maidstone. Their send-off was enthusiastic. They were *paraded inside the Drill Hall on the Pantiles, and marched from there carrying their kitbags to the South Eastern Station headed by Major Pott and the other officers. As they emerged they were greeted by salvos of cheering from the large crowd which had assembled. Flags were waved and hats flung into the air, and the Yeomen were escorted by the cheering crowd right up to the Station where the enthusiasm was doubled... The station yard, Vale-road and half-way up Mount Pleasant were thronged with a packed and excited crowd – absolutely heedless of the rain – cheering and singing patriotic songs for all they were worth.*

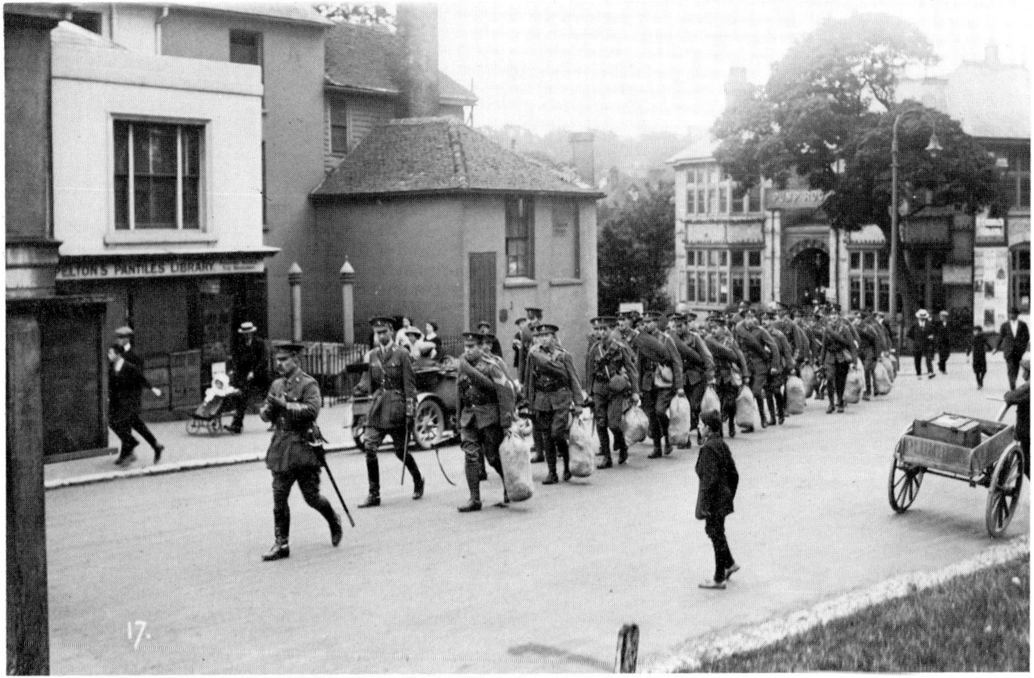

9. This and the preceding postcard were published by a local photographer as part of a series commemorating the departure of the Yeomanry on 4th August 1914. On their way from the Corn Exchange to the Central Station they marched past the Pump Room, since demolished (see No. 10) and along the back of the Pantiles. The shop on the corner, which for many years had been leased by a baker and confectioner, at this time stood vacant and remained so for several seasons; by the following year Aubrey Pelton had also closed the Library next door, though he continued operating as a stationer at premises in the High Street and on Mount Pleasant until 1934. Before the arrival of a public telephone system in Tunbridge Wells, Richard Pelton, founder of the firm, had installed his own private line between this shop on the Pantiles and his printing works in Broadway; visitors are said to have viewed it as a curiosity.

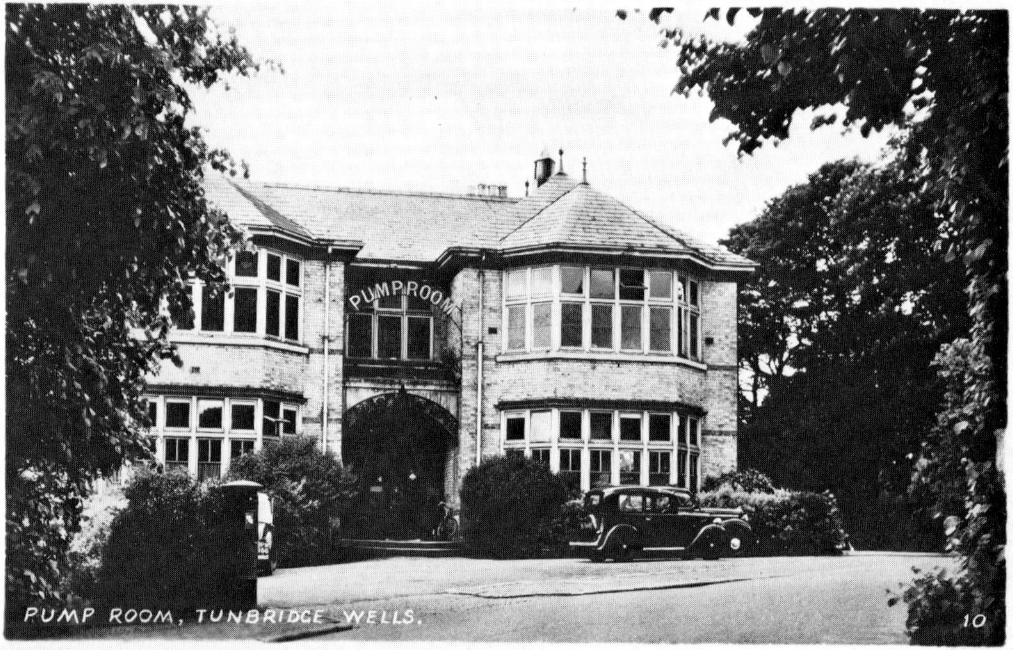

10. As facilities for visitors drinking the chalybeate water under the portico at the east end of the Pantiles had 'hitherto been somewhat meagre and primitive', a company was formed to remedy the deficiency 'as well as to provide a place of resort for social intercourse, recreation and amusement'; accordingly the Pump Room was built at the west end, the Marquess of Abergavenny laying the foundation stone on 6th November 1877. Chalybeate water was supplied from a second spring. The charge in the 1890's was two pence, which included 'entrance to the spacious and very pleasant reading room and the use of the papers, periodicals, chess, draughts, etc. upon the tables'. The Nevill Club occupied part of the premises with its own reading, billiard and smoking rooms, and there was a 'handsomely-appointed' Masonic Lodge on the first floor. In the late 1960's it was pulled down and replaced by the present Union House.

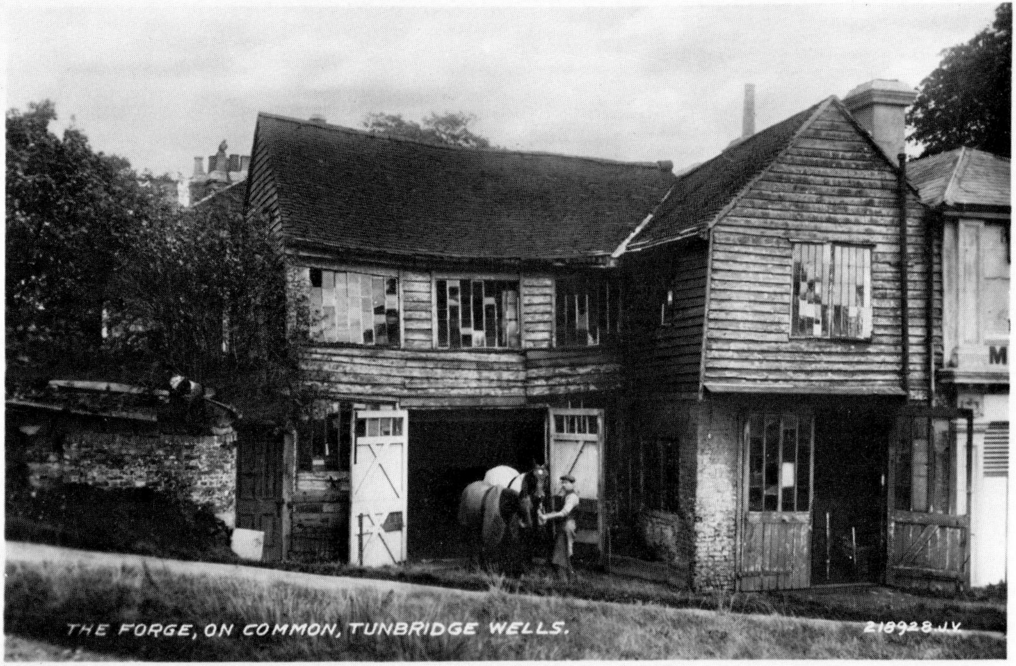

11. *Another old landmark has disappeared in the development of the town* noted an advertisement of A.E. Arthur, builder of the new Fonthill Rest Shelter in 1939. *These old forge buildings on the Common were a link with the past. Formerly a carriage works, and afterwards taken over by the Corporation and used as a temporary Fire Station and Headquarters of the old Salvage Corps, they have been demolished to make way for an up-to-date rest rooms and general conveniences. Modern architecture has been introduced in the new buildings which harmonise with the immediate surroundings. The Rest Rooms will be appreciated by all using the lovely Common.* Under the proprietorship of W.T. Noakes, the Tunbridge Wells Coach Works had been a large business with showrooms beside the old forge, turning out *broughams, landaus, phaetons, waggonettes, gigs and dog-carts, & c.,... the finish being in the best possible style for the surrounding neighbourhood.*

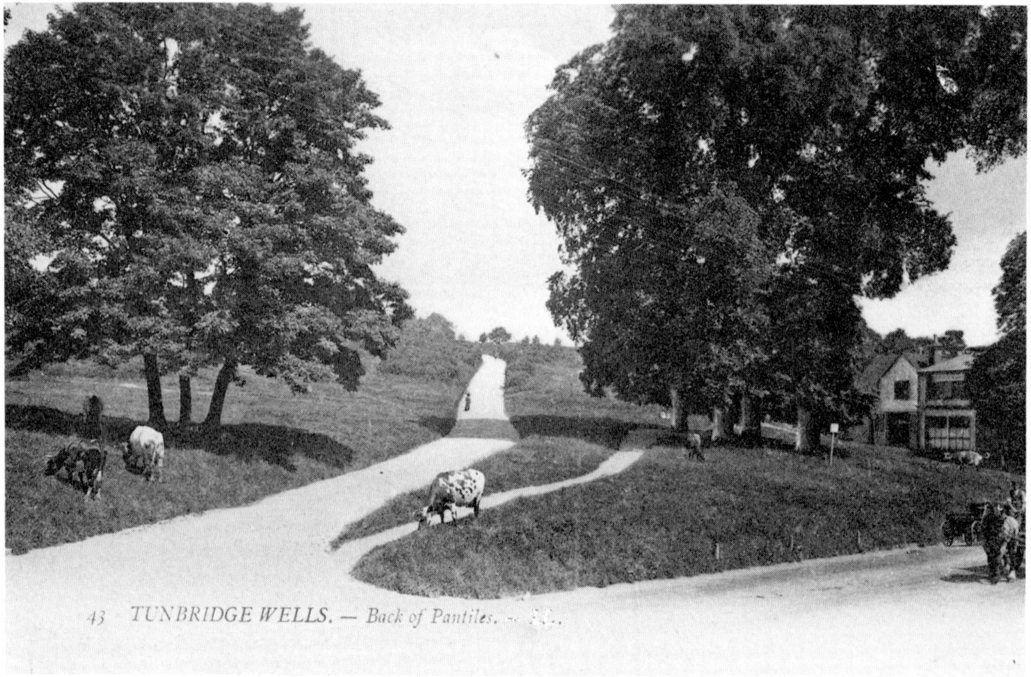

12. *The Back of the Pantiles... commands a view of the Common and of several groups of noble elm trees, unfortunately diminished in number through the violence of occasional gales from the south-west. Many young trees have quite recently been planted to replace the old,* wrote the author of a late nineteenth century local guide book. The area of Common seen in this postcard dating from the turn of the century has suffered many changes in the last eighty years. The old forge was demolished in the 1930's (see previous postcard) and woodland has gradually replaced the open heath. Following the droughts of the mid-seventies many trees on the Common succumbed; and 1977 saw the disappearance of the familiar groups of noble elms, victims of Dutch elm disease. Saplings of other species have been planted to replace this loss.

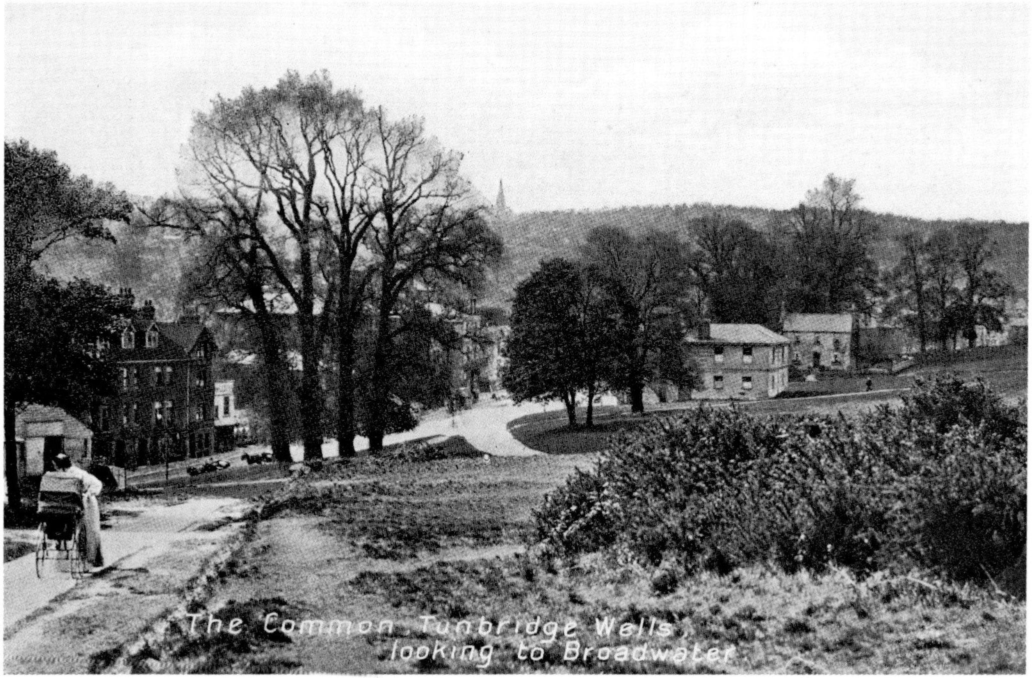

13. For years the four elms towards the centre of this Edwardian view dominated the corner of the Common opposite the Back of the Pantiles. Such a familiar landmark were they, that they acquired the affectionate appellation 'The Four Brothers' until in the early 1930's two of the group were blown down in gales, and the other two becoming unsafe were cut down. Later in the thirties, the buildings to the extreme left were demolished (see postcard No. 11) to make space for the Fonthill Rest Rooms as little construction on new sites has been allowed on the Common since the eighteenth century. Following a dispute between the freehold tenants and the Lord of the Manor of Rusthall, who having leased the land near the Wells for herbage sub-let it for building purposes, the Common was protected from further encroachment by an Act of Parliament in 1739/40.

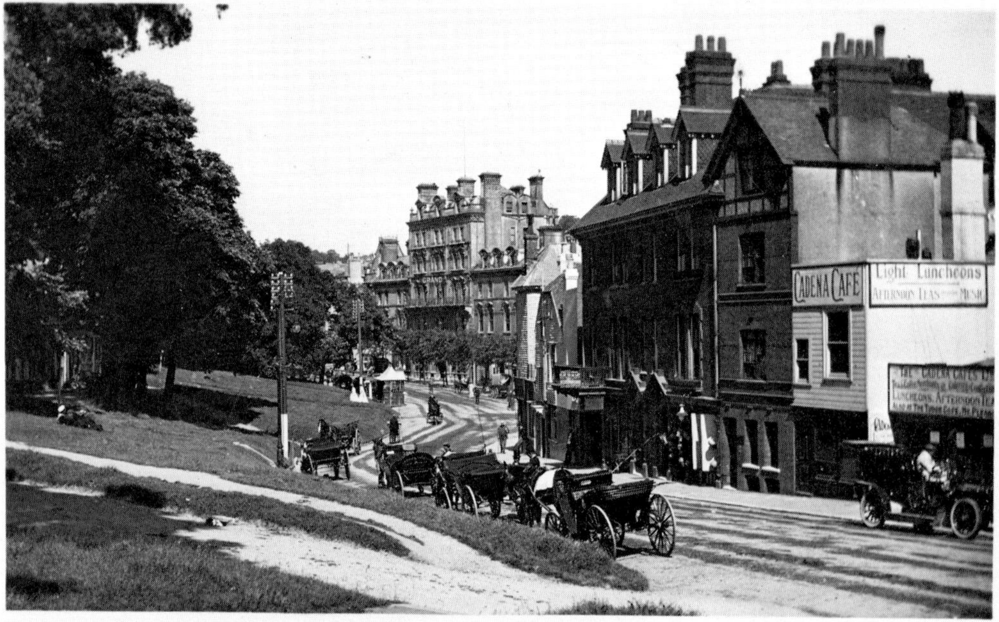

LONDON ROAD & GRAND HOTEL, TUNBRIDGE WELLS.

14. Hackney carriages such as those in the foreground of this card postmarked 1909, might be hired at any of the stands either by distance or time to any place within five miles of the General Post Office, first class fares being one shilling per mile or three shillings for an hour. First and second class carriages for five or four persons in addition to the driver were horse-drawn; small third class carriages for two persons were drawn by ponies, asses or mules. As so many cabmen had their stand at the edge of the Common, in 1908 a cabmen's shelter was erected in the London Road. About this time Lloyd's Café became The Cadena; later both parts of the building were renovated with a second storey added to the right. The restaurant seems to have closed when adjacent properties regarded by the consultant architect as beyond repair and of insufficient merit to justify 'further tinkering' were demolished in the late thirties.

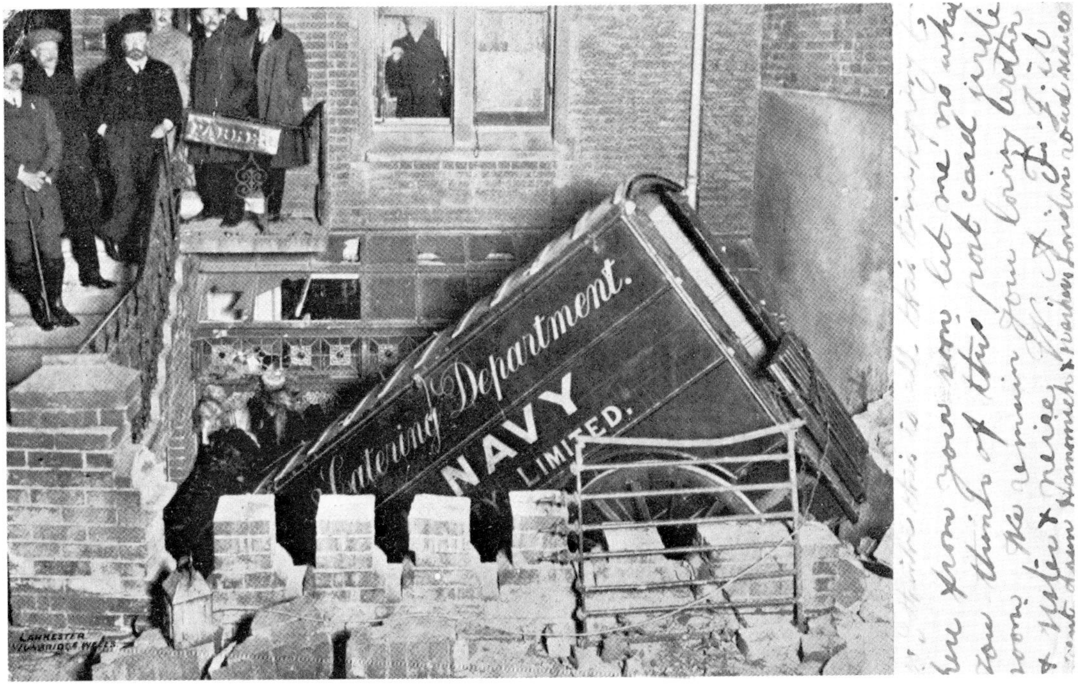

15. The enterprising photographer Percy Lankester took a flashlight picture of this 'extraordinary accident' to issue as a postcard. On the evening of 26th April 1906 *as an Army and Navy Stores pantechnicon was being driven down the steep incline of Major Yorkes-road, the driver, through imperfect skidding, lost control of the horse and van, which dashed through the railings of Messrs. Parker and Hammick's back premises (a well-known firm of caterers on the Pantiles) and fell through the stained glass roofing of the area, and jammed between the walls, while the horse was literally doubled up, with its head between its hind legs, and had to be shot... The driver... had a miraculous escape. He kept his seat and was stunned by the violence of the concussion, but on being conveyed to the hospital by the police, it was found that no bones were broken... An immense crowd during this evening witnessed the overturned van.*

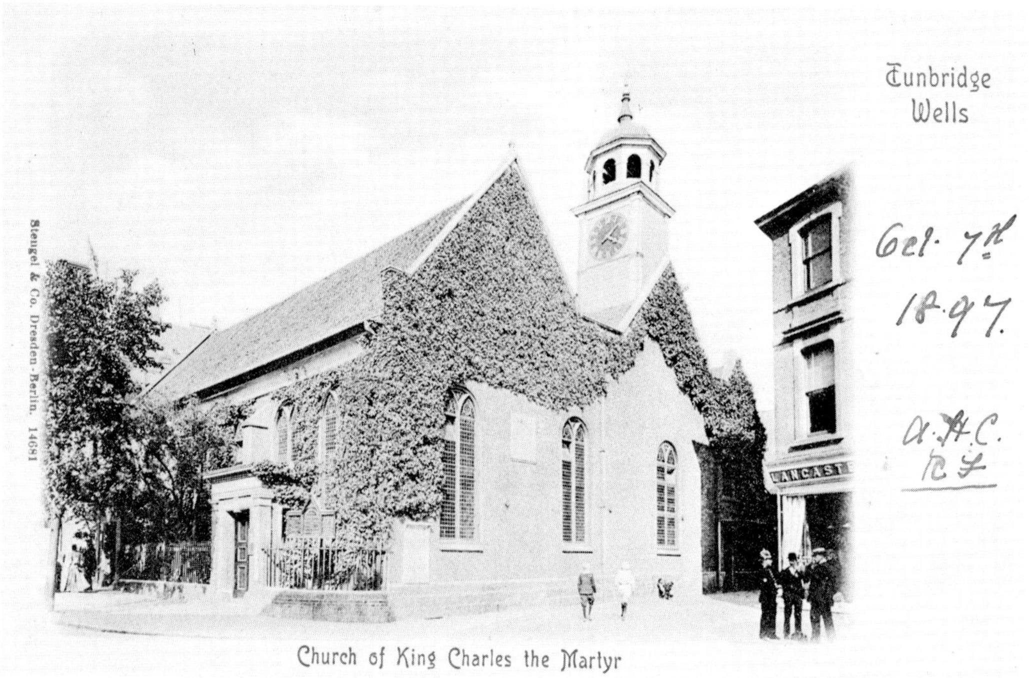

16. *On the opposite side of the road is the Chapel of Ease, the oldest Church in the town. It boasts a sun-dial, the only one, we believe, in the town. The Church has an ancient appearance as it is completely enveloped in ivy... Why it was called the Chapel of Ease, is not known as the seats are not particularly comfortable. If we had our way, the seat-makers of the country should be condemned to sit for a couple of hours every day in one of their own seats. On second thoughts, however, this would be too great a punishment, as they might be lamed for life,* wrote the author of a comic guide in 1880. Built in the last quarter of the seventeenth century as a chapel-of-ease to Tonbridge Parish Church, only in 1887 was it consecrated as a church and it acquired its own ecclesiastical district. So close did it stand to parish boundaries that tradition erroneously claimed the pulpit to be in Speldhurst, communion-table in Tonbridge and vestry in Frant.

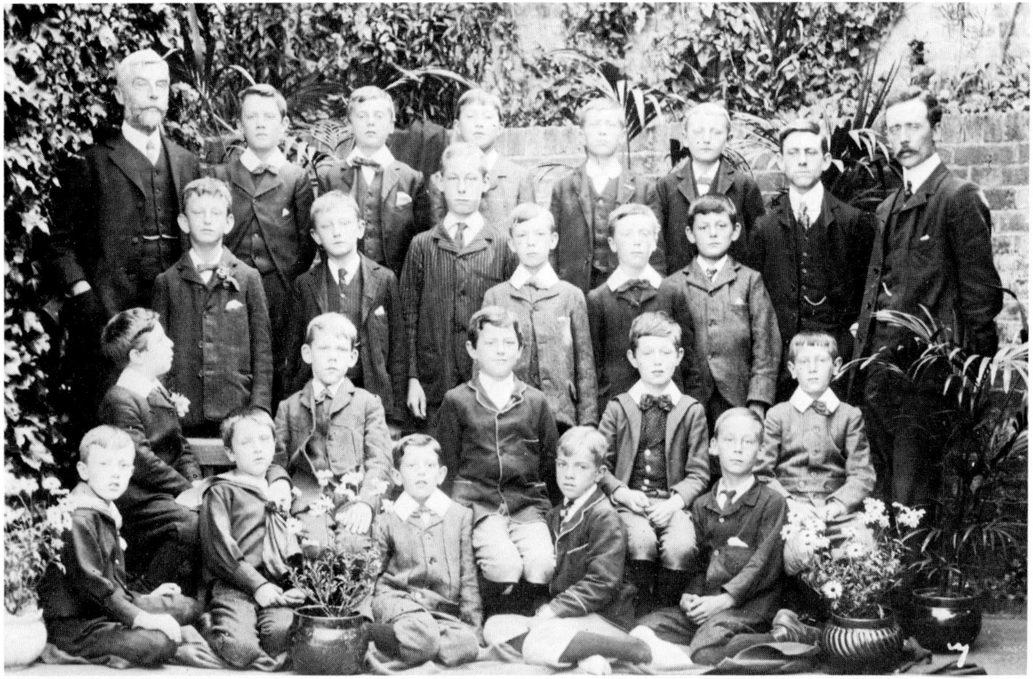

17. This postcard of about 1905 shows one of the classes of King Charles School. On his retirement in 1914 after thirty-five years as Headmaster, Mr. W.A. Diggens (on left) was described as *a born organiser and stickler for details... a thorough scholar, and a skilful imparter of knowledge. He is a firm disciplinarian but a humane and humorous master. His scripture lessons are full of profit and delight; he can read and recite with the best, he is the slacker's most pitiless foe, and so mighty a host is he in English grammar that Old Boys in writing to him from far corners of the globe thank him with the keenest relish for teaching them that 'the verb to be is never transitive'.* To the disgust of one School Inspector, who regarded them as 'of little educational value', he taught the boys shorthand and book-keeping, and in 1904 experimented with ambidextrous training, issuing copy books to all classes for practice in left-hand writing.

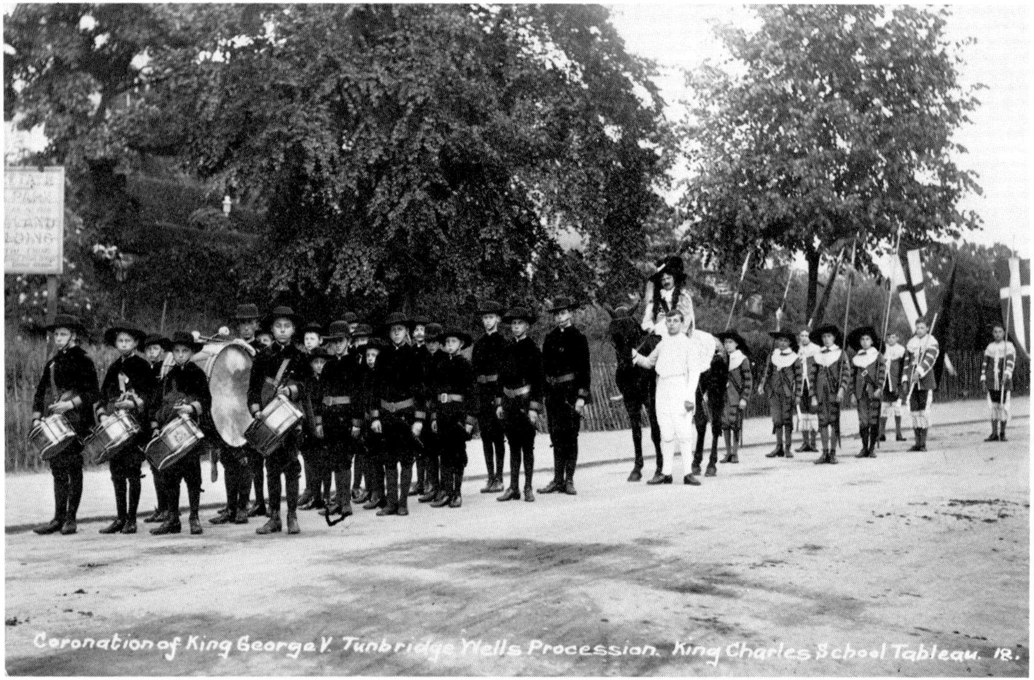

18. *Friday 23. Coronation Week,* wrote the Headmaster of King Charles School in June 1911 in the school Log Book. *On Thursday the boys assembled in school and marched to the Lower Cricket Ground to sing the National Anthem with the other children of the Borough. In the afternoon there was a procession round the Town and about 70 of our scholars represented the Entry of Charles II into London. The weather was fine until evening when there was a heavy rain. Our part of the procession was a great success.* For some weeks previous, parents had been occupied not only in making costumes for the Coronation procession, but also uniforms for the School Fife and Drum Band, which led the tableau. All the public elementary schools of the town were represented in a historical sequence of tableaux, starting with 'Caractacus in Rome' and ending with the 'Proclamation of Queen Victoria as Empress of India'.

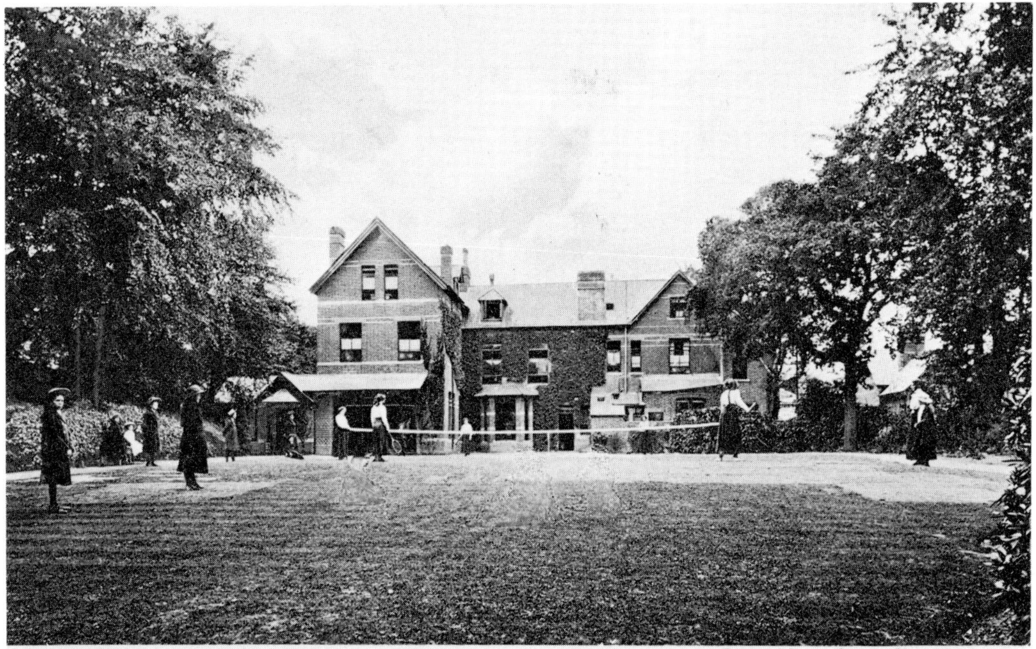

St. Clair, Tunbridge Wells. *Back View from Lawn*

19. St. Clair's ladies' school was one of the numerous private educational establishments that have abounded in Tunbridge Wells since Victorian times. About 1905 Miss Vickery took over the premises at No. 25 Frant Road from a Miss Bingley; within two years she had developed the school and acquired property in Warwick Park, to which she retired ten years later leaving the school under the charge of an unmarried relative (probably her niece), Miss C.E. Desprers Vickery. This rear view of the school from across the lawn was sent by one of the mistresses or the Matron in 1914 to a friend, explaining that she would be unable to come to Rusthall next morning as *I have two girls in the sick room & Miss Vickery will be away all day, so I must not leave.*

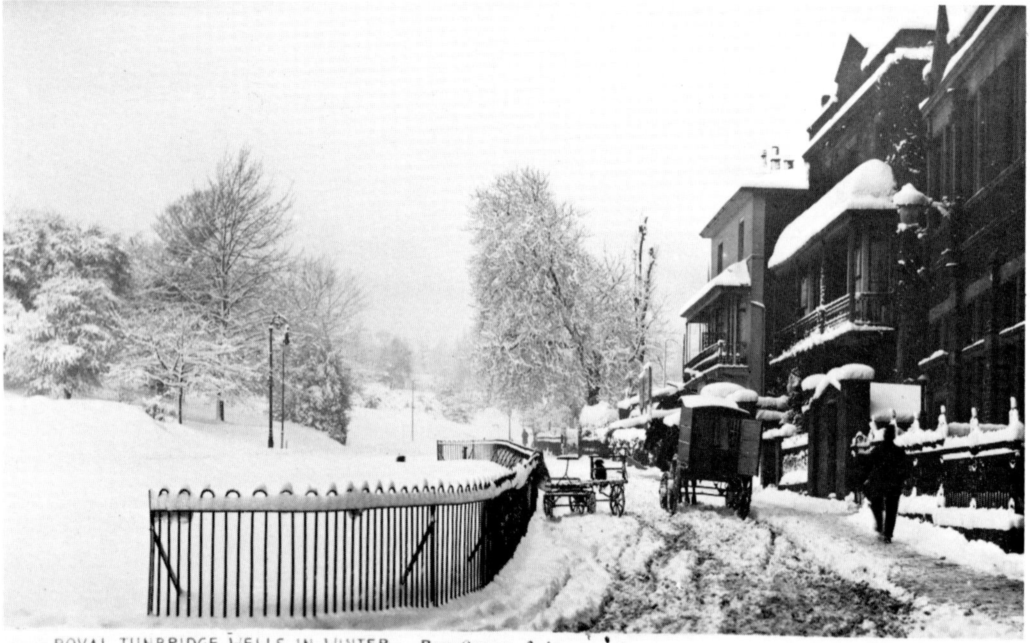

20. In the 1890's there were six houses in London Road between Vale Road and Vale Avenue; first to disappear were Bath House and South View, demolished to provide part of the site for the new General Post Office which moved from the Pantiles in 1895. It was immediately regretted that the main front had 'not been planned so that it faced the Common, it would then have formed a more imposing architectural feature'. The farther pair of houses came down shortly before the construction of the Tunbridge Wells and Counties Club in 1909, while Heath Villa and Sydenham Villa, seen here in about 1912, survived until the sixties, when the Post Office annexed the sites. At the beginning of the century, the Post Office was open daily from 7 a.m. to 10 p.m. apart from Sundays, when it opened for three hours only. Letter collections were every day from 4 a.m. until midnight, with deliveries guaranteed for the same day to much of Kent, Surrey, Sussex and London.

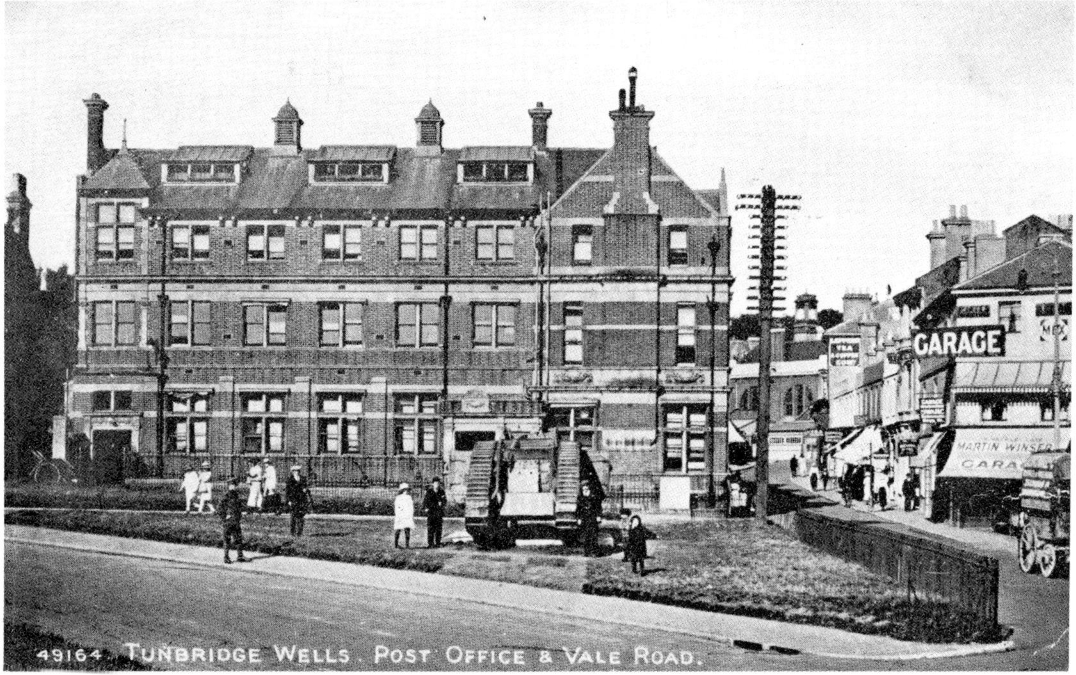

21. Between the two wars a tank stood on the green before the General Post Office, presented to the Borough by the National War Savings Committee. On 30th July 1919 it was formally received by the Mayor. A procession was arranged from the Goods Station 'where the monster had been waiting in readiness for the hour of its public appearance', and along Camden Road which had retained its peace decorations and triumphal arches. The tank had nearly completed its uneventful journey, 'it had performed no circus tricks, it had not even butted any civic dignitary marching in front of it' when it occurred to one of the Aldermen that 'the star performer of the day had not shown his capacity for climbing any obstacle in its path'. A word to the Officer in charge and 'the monster, apparently of its own volition, turned onto the Common and in its own laborious fashion proceeded to climb the steep bank... and disappeared behind the trees'.

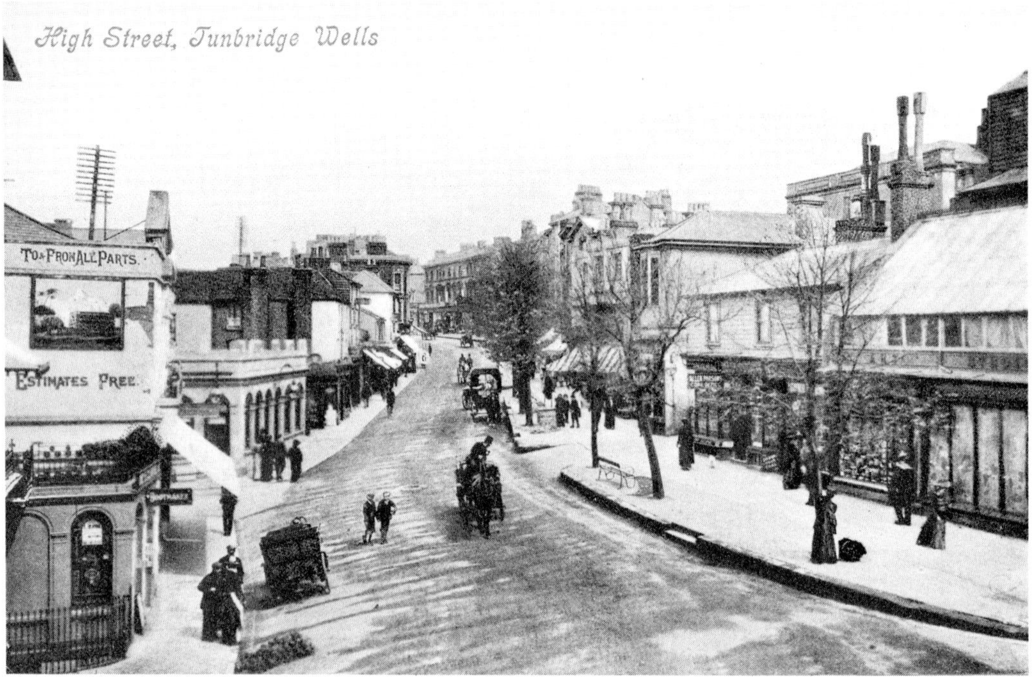

22. The central portion of the High Street has remained virtually unchanged since the beginning of the century, but more recent buildings have replaced those at the lower end below the White Bear Hotel, whose roof also has acquired a new profile. This postcard dates from between 1905 when W. Moor, bootmaker, is first recorded in trade directories as occupying the premises on the left next to Thomas White, family butcher, and 1909 when Allen Parsons' Coal Office is last mentioned at No. 77 on the right. During this time, the neighbouring Art Studio above No. 81 on the corner of Mount Sion (see next picture) was occupied by the photographer H. Seymour Cousens until 1908, and afterwards by T. Doyle Rowe.

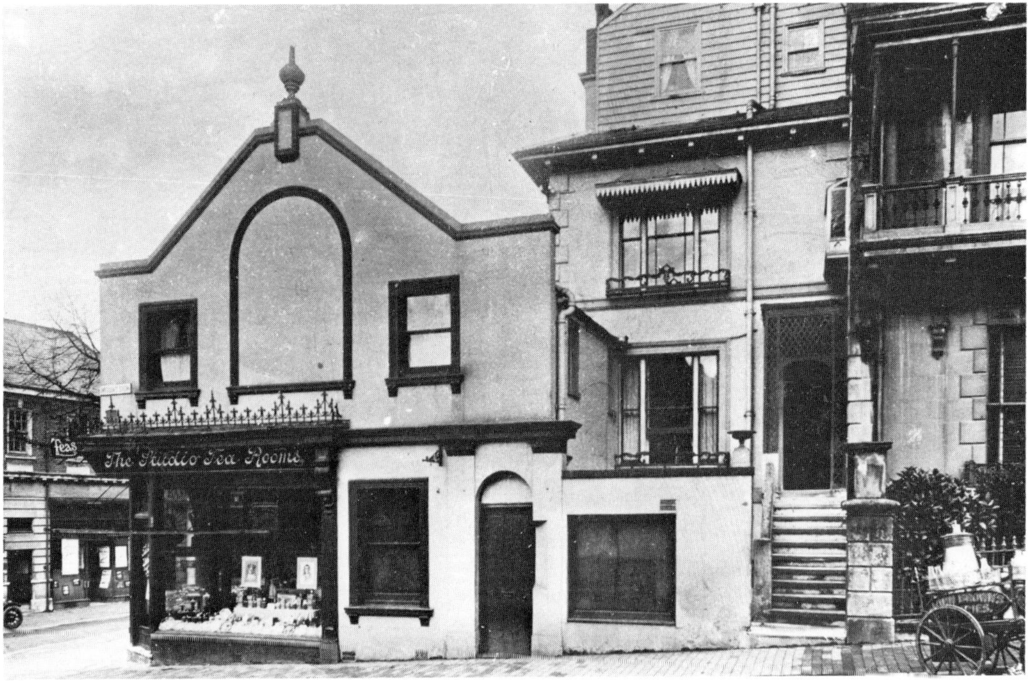

23. This view dates from about 1926 shortly before The Studio Tea Rooms in the High Street and adjacent house No. 1 Mount Sion were both demolished and the National Provincial (later Westminster) Bank constructed at the site. The latter was opened 5th May 1929. Mrs. Holroyd's Tea Rooms below the old Art Studio only occupied the premises for a couple of years. Prior to that, there was a series of photographers at both addresses including G.H. Lawrence in the 1860's, W.H. Luck and V. Hubert in the 1890's, T. Doyle Rowe, photographer and miniature painter, just before the First World War and finally Cornelius Summerfield. By the kerb outside Sion Terrace, which still exists, is one of John Brown's Dairies delivery carts; as late as this, milk was sold by the roundsman from the churn as well as delivered in bottles.

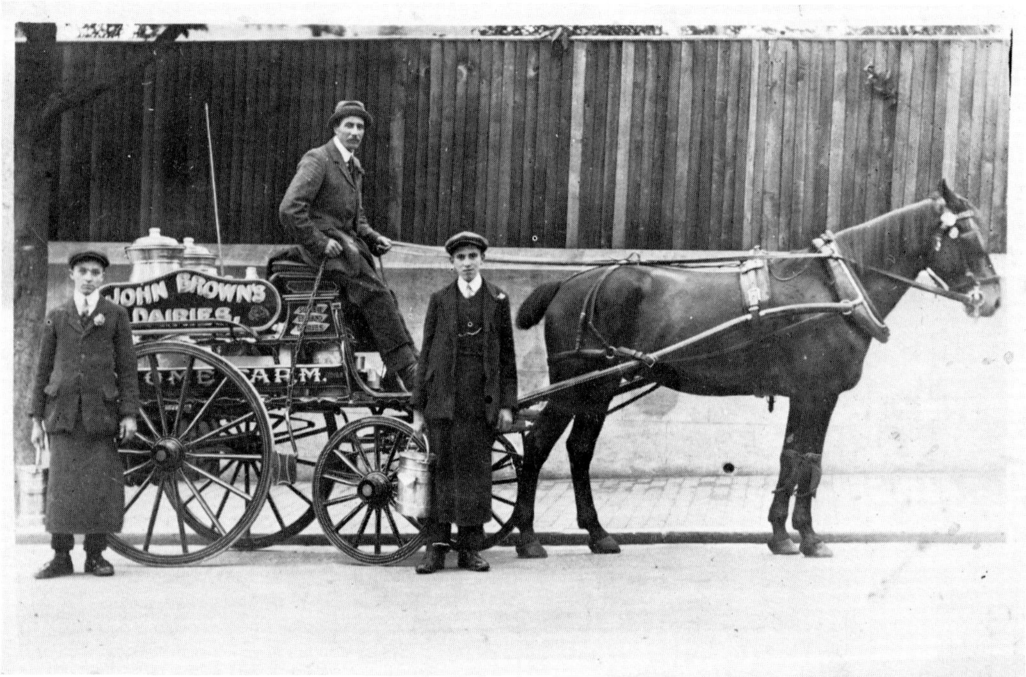

24. For many years after this postcard dating from the turn of the century, the roundsman of John Brown's Dairies made his deliveries in a horse-drawn cart. An advertisement of 1896 boasted of *A Few Facts & Advantages that Patrons have of John Brown's Dairy Produce – Firstly: Specially Appointed Sanitation Inspection by Mr. Richard Roberts, Veterinary Surgeon, Tunbridge Wells. Secondly: Selected Cows and Special Feeding. Thirdly: A Herd of Sixty Cows to be seen at Ramslye Farm, two minutes' walk from Broadwater Down, and Home Farm, Tunbridge Wells. Fourthly: Milk can be delivered from above Herd within ten minutes from time of Milking to any part of the Town. Fifthly: The Best Fitted Dairy and Butter Factory in Tunbridge Wells, with latest improvements and Steam Power. And lastly, but not least, John Brown's Twenty-Fourth Year of Personal Superintendence.* The dairy factory itself was situated on Mount Sion, with an office in the High Street.

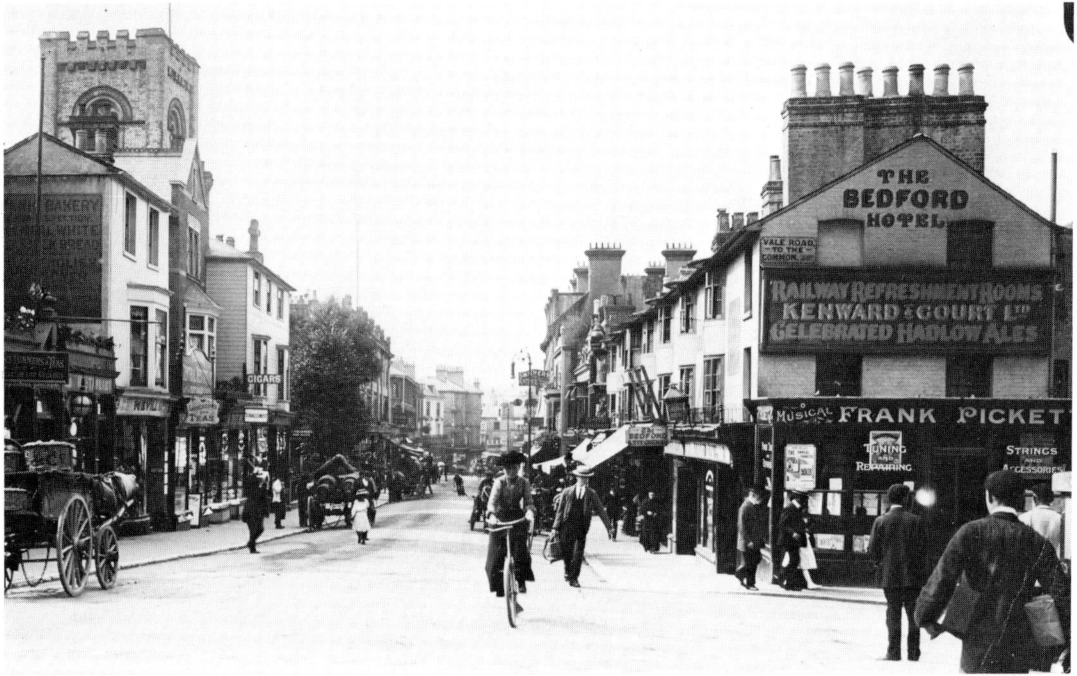

25. The most popular view of the High Street, this card dates from 1906 when the shops on the left were occupied by E. Maynard's Dining Rooms (Nos. 1, 3), The Nevill Bakery (No. 5), C. Ferrari's Central Café (No. 7), Harvey Williams, tobacconist (No. 9), Scotch Wool & Hosiery Stores (No. 11) and C. Faulkner, wine merchant (No. 13). Conspicuous is the absence of the glass superstructure above Maynard's, as it was not until the twenties that John Brown, then proprietor of the Nevill Bakery, acquired the old orangery from Hever Castle. Too long for the proposed site, it was divided into two sections, the one set in the elevated position it now occupies, the other added as a porch to one of the houses in Warwick Park. A year or so after the photograph was taken the corner of Vale Road was altered considerably when the new railway bridge was constructed, the road widened and the Bedford Hotel and adjacent shops rebuilt with their present gabled façade.

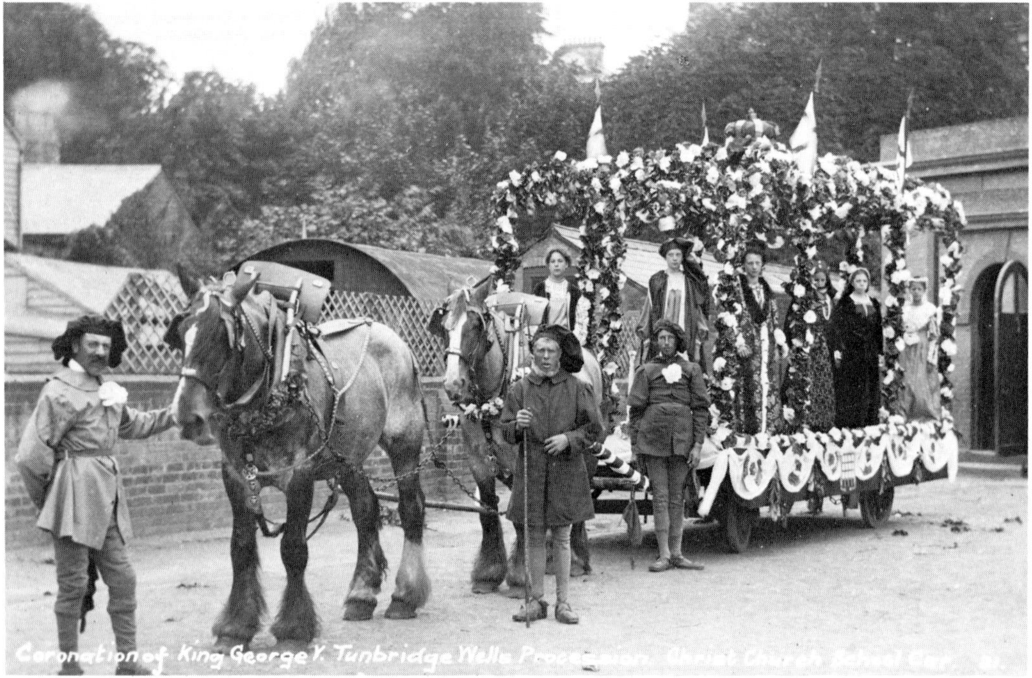

26. Celebrations in Tunbridge Wells of the Coronation of George V and Queen Mary on 22nd June 1911 began with the Ringing of Joy Bells at St. Peter's Church, the singing of the National Anthem by a special choir on Calverley Parade, Church parade at Holy Trinity and a 'Great United Meeting' on the Common. Later in the day was a 'Monster Grand Procession' through the town, 'Old English Sports' on the Lower Cricket Ground and in the evening, a magnificent firework display. The parents and pupils of Christ Church School for Girls and Infants in Vale Road, whose playground was adjacent to the Railway Station approach, prepared a car to take part in the procession decorated with white and red roses of the Houses of York and Lancaster, the Tudor rose and flags of St. George, to illustrate 'The Union of the Rival Roses'. Characters in period costume represented Henry VII and Elizabeth of York with two courtiers and ladies-in-waiting.

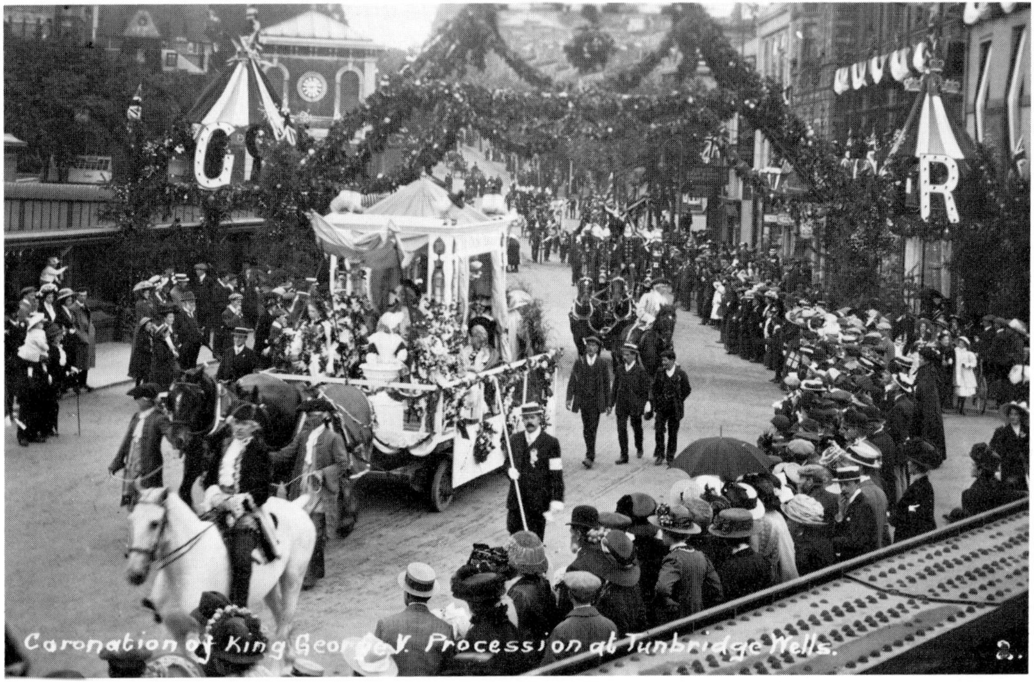

27. Referring to this section of the procession, the official programme of arrangements to celebrate the Coronation of George V, reads: *Tunbridge Wells Tradesmen's Association – 'Ye Olde Wells': Descriptive Car with carved and gorgeously coloured trellis work, surmounted by cupolas, built in the pseudo-Moorish style afterwards favoured by George IV, when Prince of Wales. Representing: Distinguished visitors being served with the chalybeate waters on the ancient Walks known as Ye Pantyles, in the year 1698. Figures: Richard Nash, popularly called 'Beau Nash' then a young man and leader of the fashionable world, handing a glass of water to Princess Anne of Denmark (afterwards Queen of England). Dipper taking water from a replica of the original basin set up at Coldbath in 1708. At each corner of the car are children suitably attired to depict the particular glories of Kent – the Garden of England – Flowers, Fruit, Hops, Corn.*

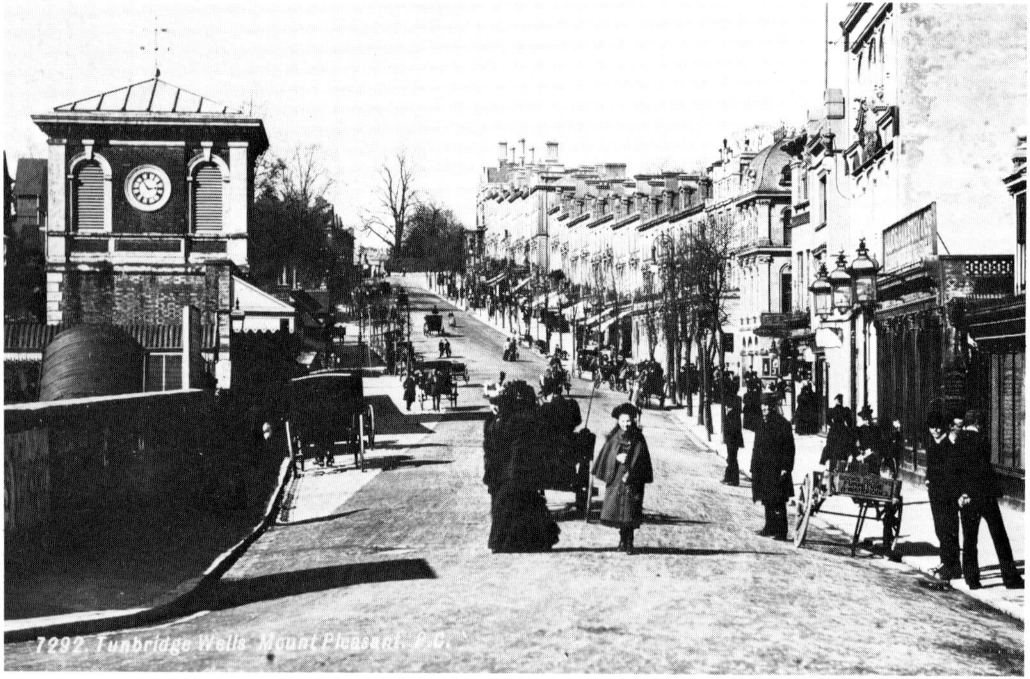

28. *It was never a thing of beauty. For years it had been regarded as the most inconvenient thing the town possessed, and with the birth of the motor car era it developed into a positive danger,* wrote a journalist of the old High Street Bridge seen here on the left. Built in 1851, improvements to the bridge were discussed as early as 1878, the Town wanting to replace it, the Railway Company obdurant. In 1905 it was declared unsafe and temporarily strengthened with timber baulks. *An up-to-date Horatius in the form of a Policeman held the bridge, and for a time had to submit to a good deal of badinage.* All vehicles had to *proceed at walking pace. It is even alleged that a costermonger whose barrow contained a couple or so of cabbages was remonstrated with because his donkey would persist in trotting over the bridge.* The next view, photographed shortly after its opening on 16th May 1907, shows the new bridge with the road widened.

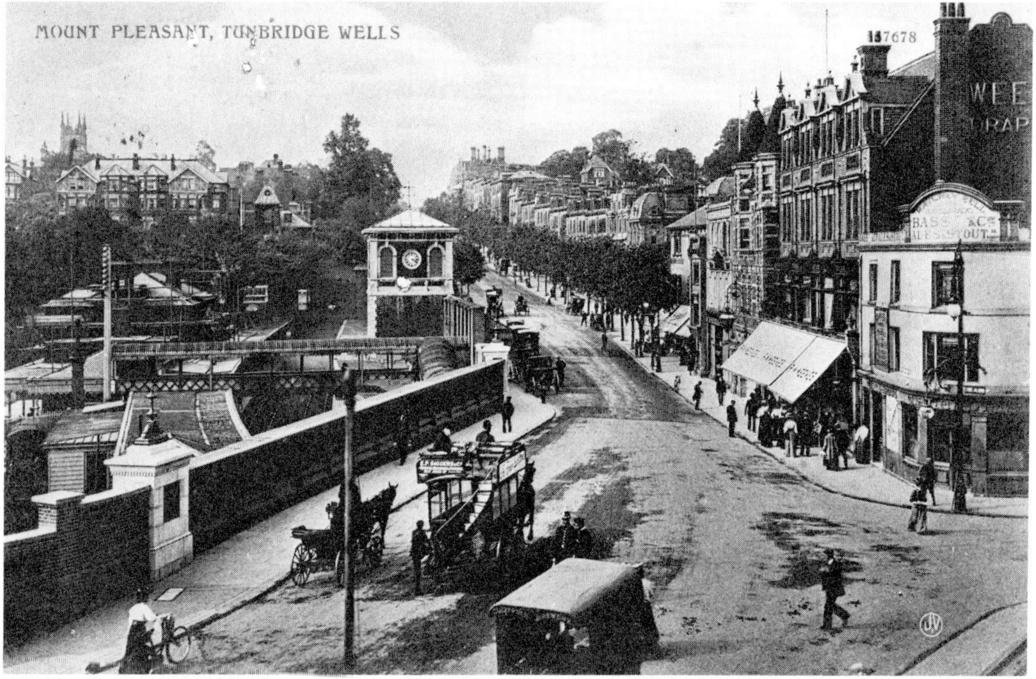

29. The old downside railway station dating from the middle of the nineteenth century was demolished a few years after this photograph and replaced by the present building designed by A.W. Blomfield. On 25th November 1912 the ceremonial starting of the clock, which the Railway Company had provided 'out of the generosity of its official heart', was preceded by the discharge of three fog signals. On the extreme right of the previous card of about 1890 is the original shop of R.W. Weekes, draper, next to the Bridge Tavern, before its rebuilding as a multi-storied hotel. By this time Weekes, draper, tailor, clothier, outfitter and boot and shoe dealer, occupied all the premises between the Railway Bell on the corner and the Bridge, as well as Nos. 7 and 9 beyond. In 1911 Weekes took over and demolished the Railway Bell Hotel in order to construct the present building; and in the late 1930's bought up the Bridge Hotel, which was likewise pulled down.

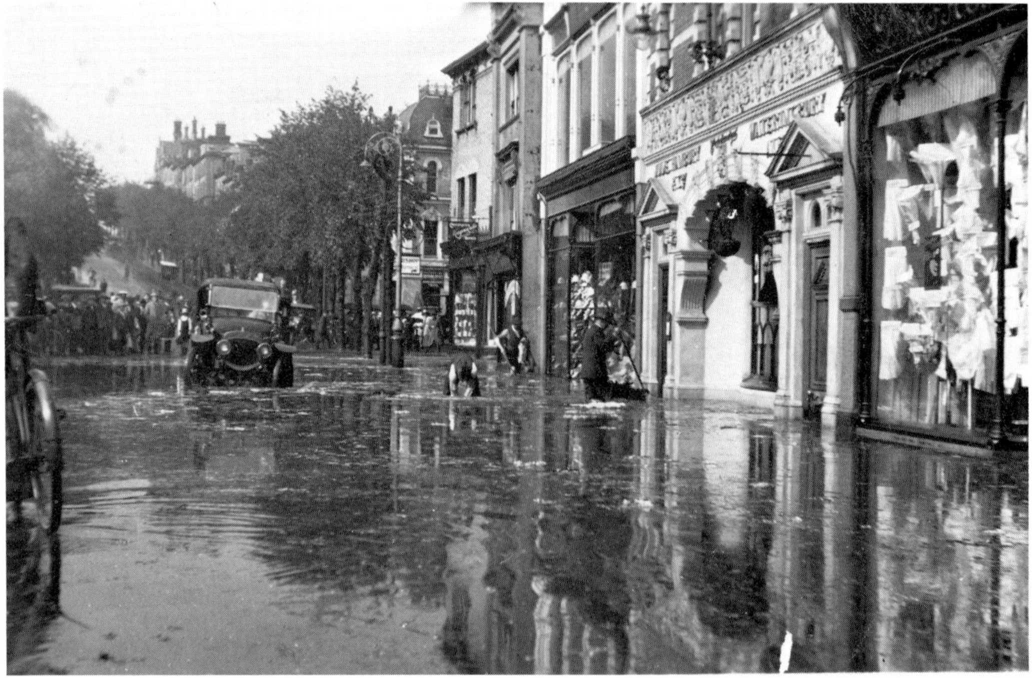

30. On 25th May 1922 *A thunder shower suddenly turned to a deluge of hail, and the gutters of the main thoroughfare were soon swiftly flowing rivulets which the gulleys could not carry off... Messrs. Weekes' corner was soon impassable, and the flood steadily rose over the pavement and invaded the ground floors of all the business premises of the Broadway and flooded the basements and cellarage. Pedestrians who had helter-skelter sought the nearest refuge from the hail, found their retreat cut off,... as the water rose to a height of two feet. The scene at Mount Pleasant during the few minutes that the storm was at its height was an exciting one. Drivers struggled with terrified horses which were stung by hailstones as big as pigeon eggs. Motor cars which essayed to pass through the flood were in one or two cases unable to get through, as the water rose above the engine; and they were stranded till the water subsided.*

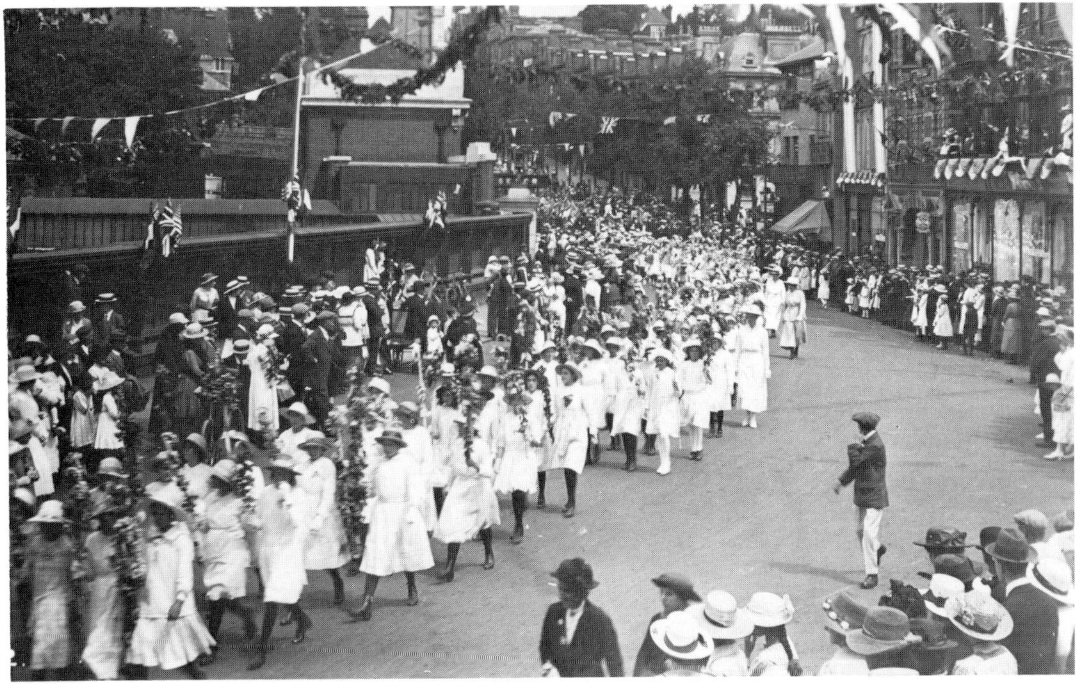

31. *Nothing prettier could be desired than the long line of schoolgirls dressed in white and each carrying either a garland tied with streamers or a basket of flowers as a posy. The cumulative effect of this profusion of flowers was generally admired, and the preparation of the multicoloured garlands must have involved an immense amount of labour as well as a heavy toll upon the floral wealth of local gardens* – so a contemporary described the children who took part in the Peace Procession of 19th July 1919. The *eventful day was ushered in at eight o'clock in the morning by a joy peal on the bells of St. Peter's... a short choral service of praise and thanksgiving was held at King Charles Church,* then the procession, one of the largest the Borough had ever witnessed, was marshalled at Grosvenor Bridge and proceeded along the decorated thoroughfares of the town to the Lower Cricket Ground for a short memorial service.

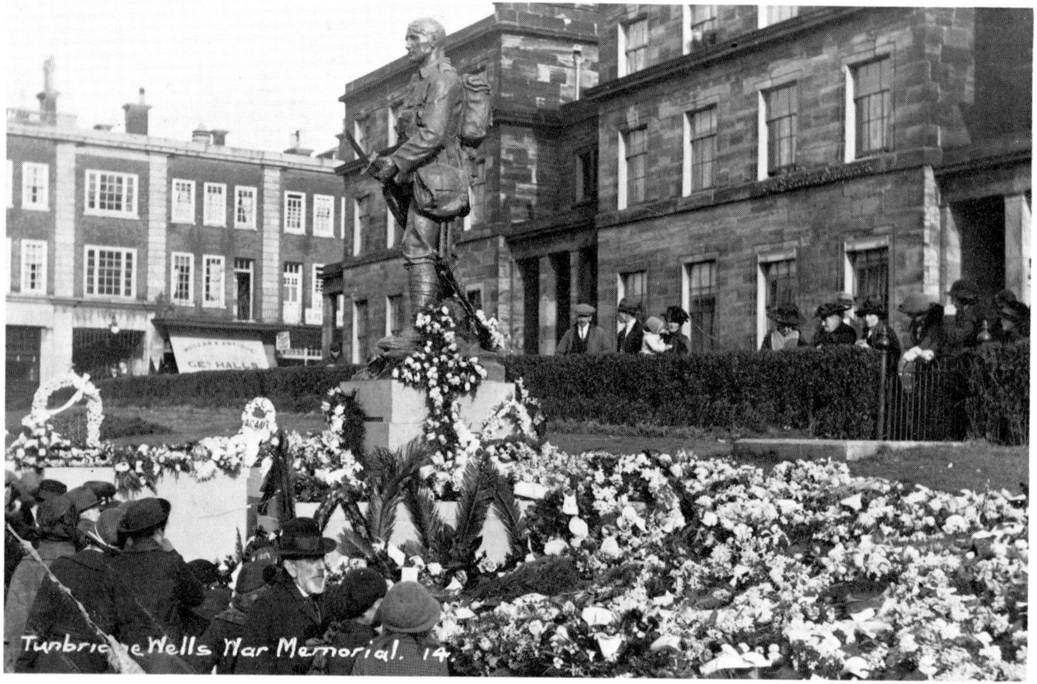

32. In 1919 a meeting was held to consider the provision of a War Memorial, but not until 11th February 1923 did the unveiling take place, *a singularly beautiful and appropriate ceremony, simple, dignified and touching, and it will live long in the memories of the vast concourse of persons who attended to do reverence to the occasion.* The *bronze figure of a khaki hero, fully equipped for the fray and combined in the facial expression of which is both tenderness and determination* was the work of S. Nicholson Babb. Colonel Viscount Hardinge performed the unveiling, the Guard of Honour was furnished by the 4th Battalion, The Queen's Own Royal West Kent Regiment, and the Boy Scouts, Girl Guides, Sea Scouts, the Fire Brigades, Special Constables and St. John Ambulance Brigade were in attendance. Floral tributes were laid by friends and relatives of the dead. From the roof of a house in Calverley Parade, buglers sounded the 'Last Post' and 'Reveille'.

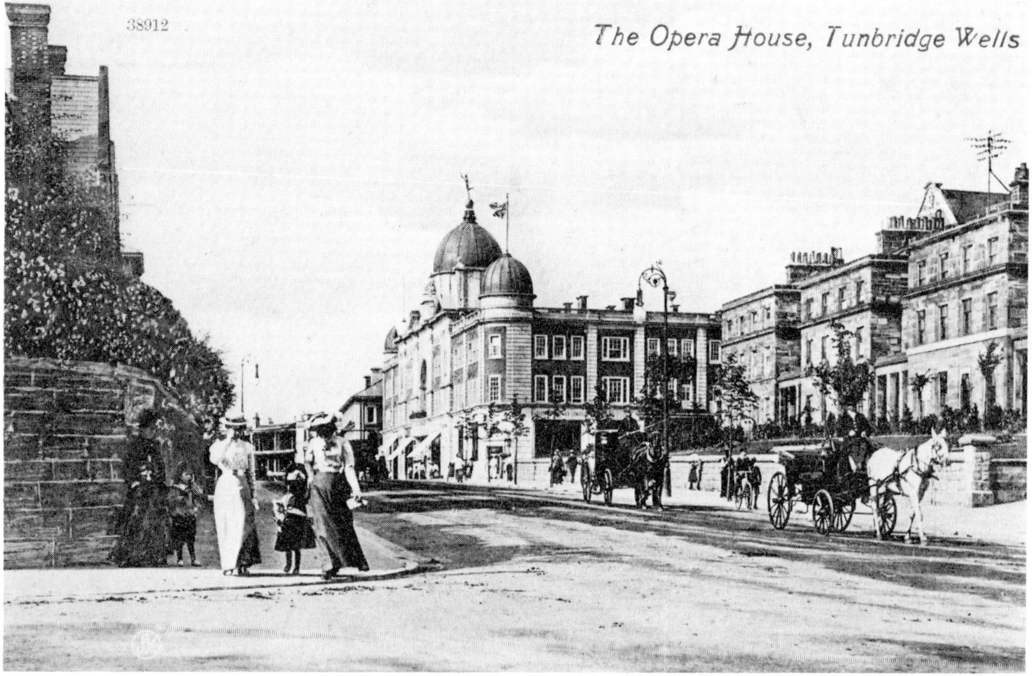

33. Calverley Parade to the right of the Opera House built to Decimus Burton's design in 1834 was demolished a century later. As early as 1895 the Council acquired the first piece of land on the site, but only after the purchase of the adjacent Calverley Terrace property was the nationwide competition held for a Civic Centre design. The Police Station and Assembly Hall were completed in 1939, the Town Hall in 1941 and the Library building in 1952. For a short period, Nos. 5-6 Calverley Parade were occupied by the Municipal Telephonic System, the first municipal system in England. Dissatisfaction with the National Telephone Company's service led to the Corporation being granted a licence in 1900. The system was inaugurated 27th July 1901, but operating costs and non-realisation of estimated revenue caused the Council to surrender the licence on 10th October 1903 and sell the exchange.

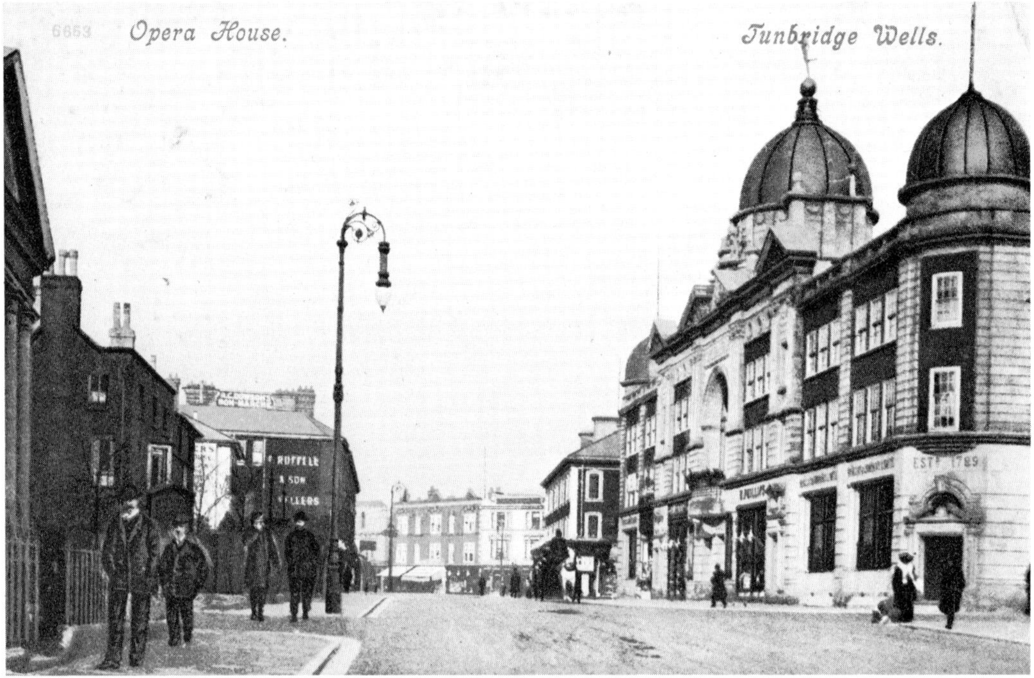

34. In June 1897 a Company was formed and the site chosen for the construction of an Opera House to commemorate Queen Victoria's Diamond Jubilee. After John P. Briggs' designs had been modified to harmonise with new municipal buildings in the vicinity, foundation stones were laid on 10th October 1901 by the Mayor, the Chairman of the Opera House Company and Sir Herbert Beerbohm Tree, who sadly did not live to fulfil his promise of acting in the theatre when opened a year later. Although called an Opera House to avoid offence, it was intended as 'a thoroughly high class Building for Concerts and Theatrical Performances'; but if its name gave no offence, the naked statue of Mercury on the central cupola certainly did and was eventually relegated to a basement. In its heyday many famous artistes performed in the Opera House; later in the 1930's the theatre was replaced by cinema and since 1968 it has functioned as a Bingo Hall.

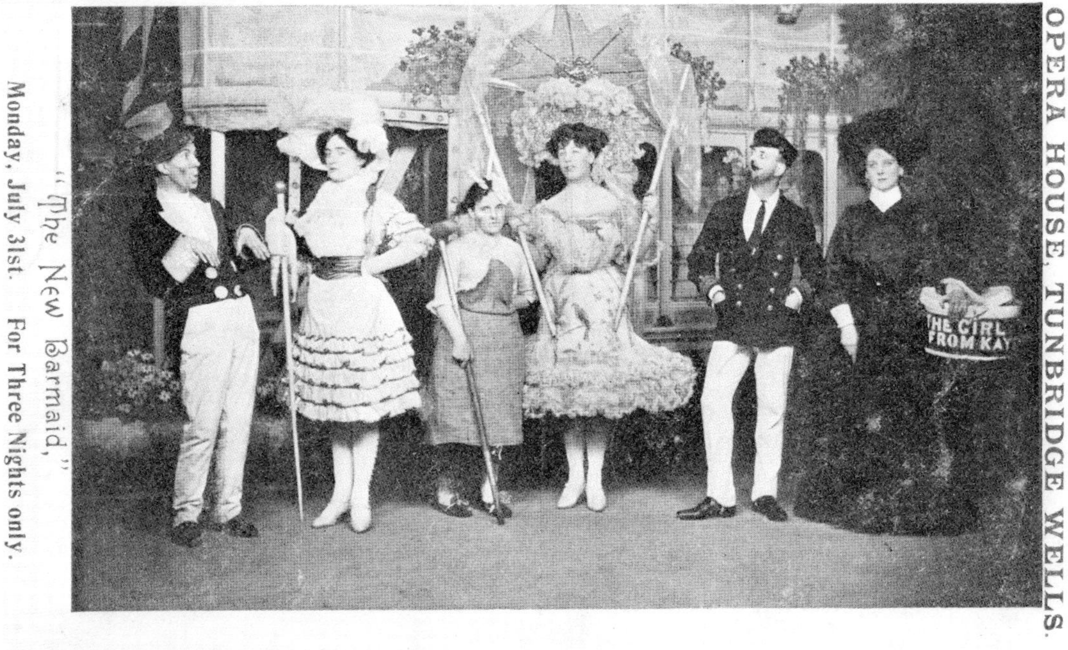

35. It was customary up to the 1920's for touring companies to publish postcards of their productions overprinted with particulars of local theatres and performance dates. Provincial managers used them as additional advertising. 'The New Barmaid', full of 'bright and tuneful music, humorous songs, graceful dances and pretty costumes' proved so popular in June 1905 that when after a short closure the Opera House reopened under the new management of Mr. C.O. Carey, the musical comedy was revived to play to appreciative audiences. The plot involves a much-tried heroine the new barmaid ultimately revealed as an heiress who marries the man of her heart. In this scene characters in carnival dress pose by a Thames houseboat. The show's highlight was a song sung by Mr. J.B. Montagu as Bertie White the waiter 'A little bit of sugar for the bird', with extra verses alluding to the new South Eastern Bridge and other local topics.

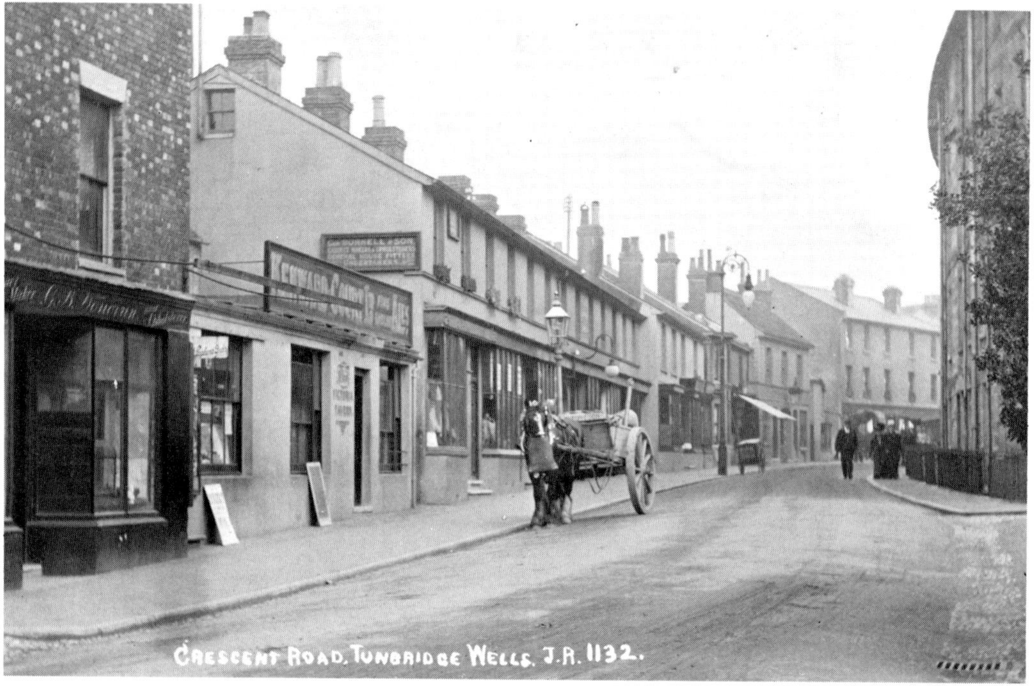

36. In the late fifties and early sixties all the terrace shops at this end of Crescent Road were demolished, as well as Holly Bank Terrace and Crescent Cottages that lay behind. The area now forms the entrance to the multi-storey car park. Around the turn of the century, G.B. Donovan, cabinet maker and furniture restorer, occupied No. 22 on the extreme left. Established in 1879, the firm operated at that address for over forty years from about 1896. Next to him was a bookbinder and printer. Beyond was the Victoria Tavern run by various managers from about 1894 to 1916. Kenward & Court, whose advertisement hoarding appears above the Tavern, had their brewery at Hadlow and a brewery store in Tunbridge Wells High Street from at least 1886. At No. 25 George Burnell & Son, described in trade directories as blindmakers, continued until the beginning of the First World War. No. 30 onwards and Calverley Crescent opposite still exist.

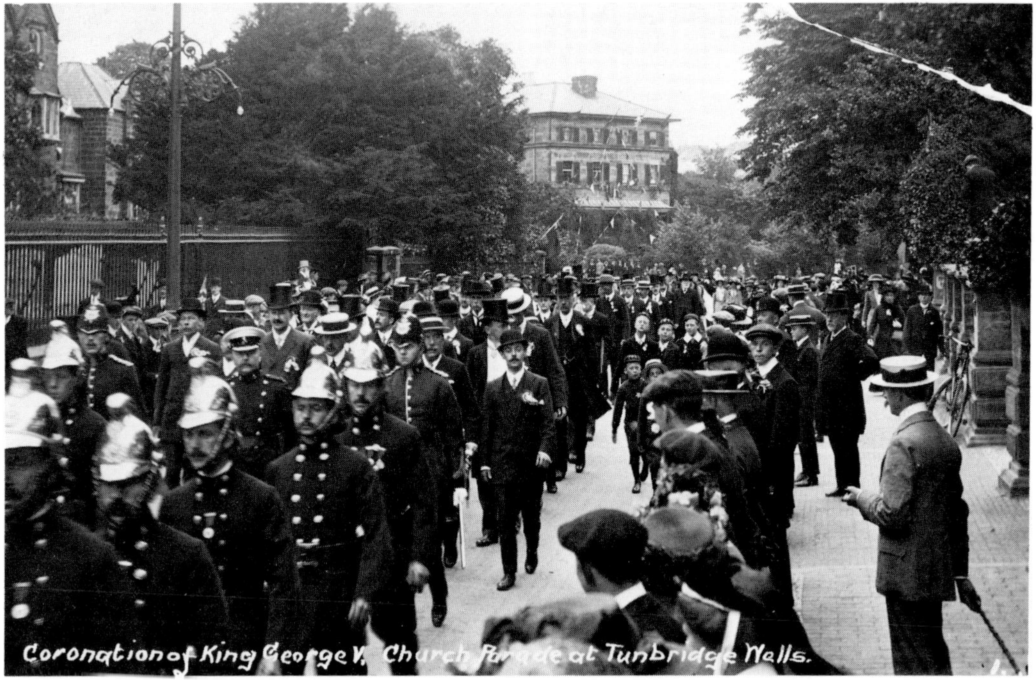

37. Services were held in most places of worship in Tunbridge Wells on Thursday 22nd June 1911 to celebrate the Coronation of George V and Queen Mary. The Church Parade at Holy Trinity was *attended by the Mayor, Aldermen, Councillors and Magistrates, in State, the Coronation Committee and a detachment of the Yeomanry and Territorials with the Cyclist Corps accompanied by the splendid Band of the 6th Battalion Royal Fusiliers.* The Fire Brigade, seen here passing the railings of the Priory, were also in attendance. Decorated with bunting for the occasion, Calverley Mount on the corner of Mount Pleasant opposite the end of Church Road was at this time occupied by R. Vaughan Gower (solicitor, later Mayor of Tunbridge Wells) and the Tunbridge Wells Football Club. Designed by Decimus Burton in the 1830's, it was pulled down a century later to provide a site for the central portion of the present Town Hall.

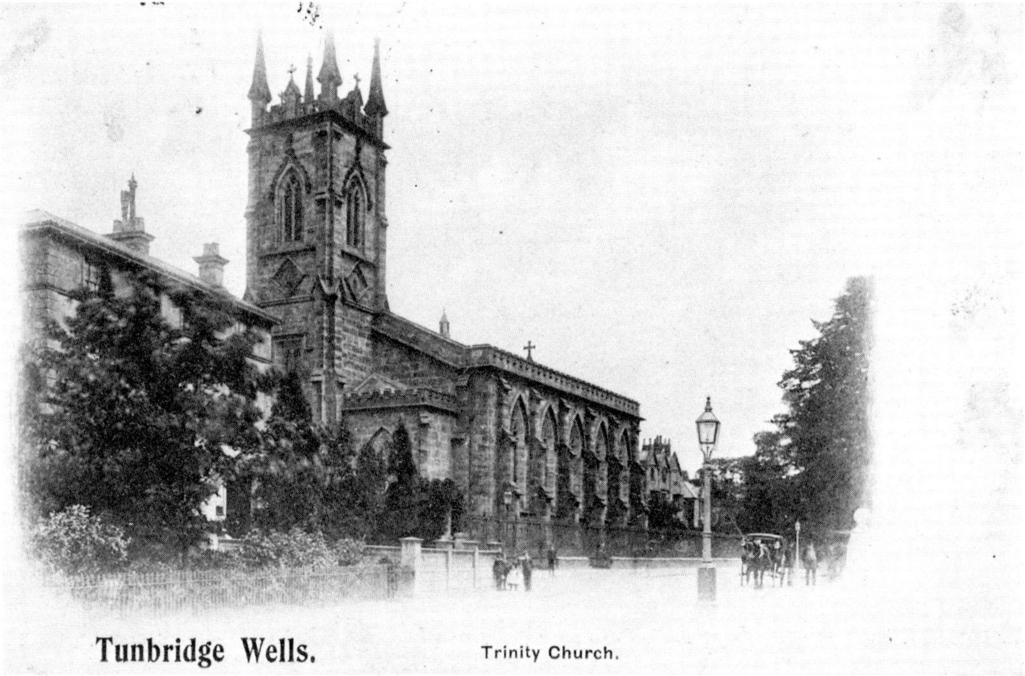

38. George V's Coronation was also celebrated with illuminations. *A brilliant effect was produced on the massive square tower of Holy Trinity Church by a lavish use of electric glow lamps in many colours. The lights were placed closely together in rows round various parts of the tower, and especially pretty was the effect produced by the illumination of the railings, trellis work, and other carved masonry. Many of the lamps hung in festoons from the centre to the four corners of the tower, which was simply ablaze with many-hued light after dusk. The splendid illuminations made Trinity Church tower a distinctive Tunbridge Wells landmark for miles around.* The most famous piece of Decimus Burton's architecture in the town, Holy Trinity was consecrated in 1829 and declared redundant in 1974. Public support for the Appeal saved it from demolition and enabled work to start on converting the church into an Arts Centre.

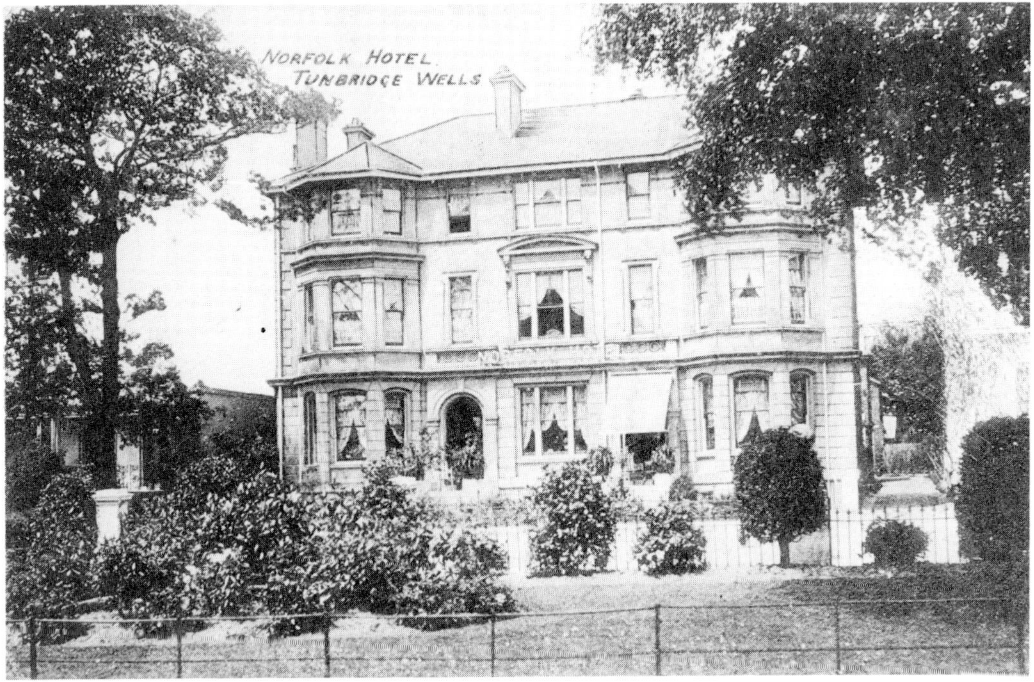

39. The late nineteenth century view of Holy Trinity Church on the previous postcard shows No. 8 Church Road, confusedly known at various times as Dorset Villa, Dorset House and Dorset Lodge; pulled down in the late fifties, its site is now occupied by a bank. Next door, Nos. 10-12 Dorset Place (part of which was also once called Dorset House) and No. 14, of which the first building on the site was the original Dorset House, were demolished in the early sixties to make space for Telephone House, the administrative headquarters of the Tunbridge Wells Telephone Area which opened in 1965. The Norfolk Hotel, formerly Pangbourne House which replaced the old Dorset House at No. 14, functioned for fifty years from about 1909. In this view, postmarked 1911, the hotel is seen soon after opening; in later years a glass porch was added between the bay windows, otherwise its external appearance remained almost unchanged until the end.

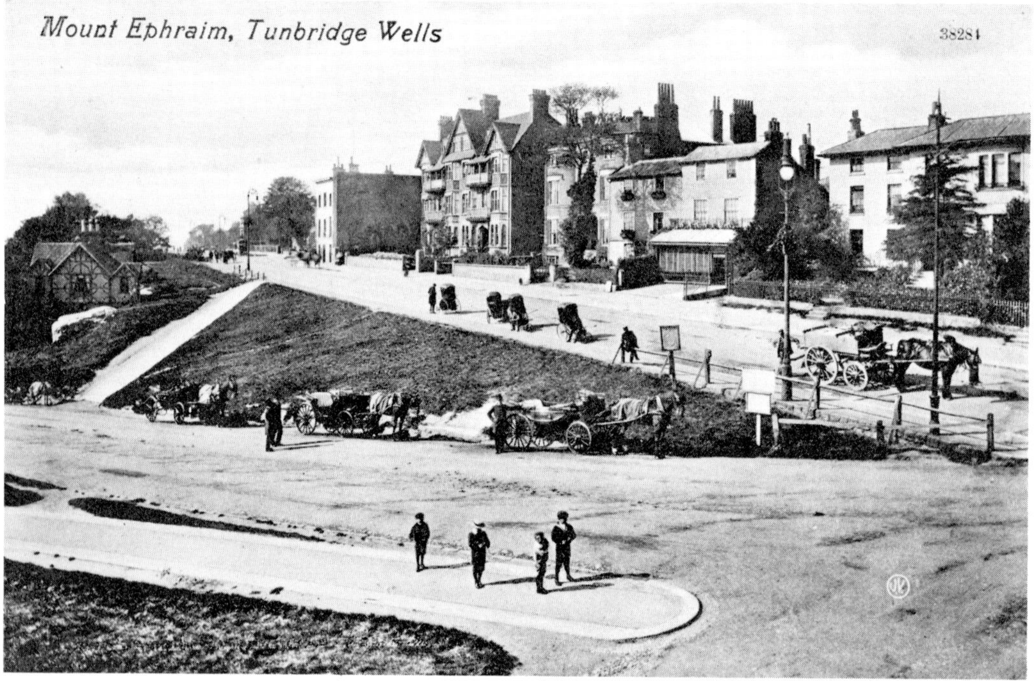

40. *Pony carriages with invalids, the broughams of medical men, ladies and gentlemen on horseback, barouches bearing ineffable dowagers, lastly a grand landau with two splendid white horses and servants in grand liveries, the equipage containing, it was whispered, a Duchess,* wrote the Holiday Correspondent of the Daily Telegraph in 1879, *These were signs unmistakable that we were entering the precincts of Tunbridge Wells the Fashionable, the Cheerful, the Salubrious.* The confluence of London Road and Mount Ephraim was traditionally the stand for Bathchairs and carriages awaiting hire. Opposite, Buckingham House, in later years a private hotel, was demolished in the mid-twenties to make way for the outlet of Royal Chase. For many years around the turn of the century the Warwick family were butchers at No. 52; in the forties when it reverted to a private house, the projecting shop front and forecourt were removed.

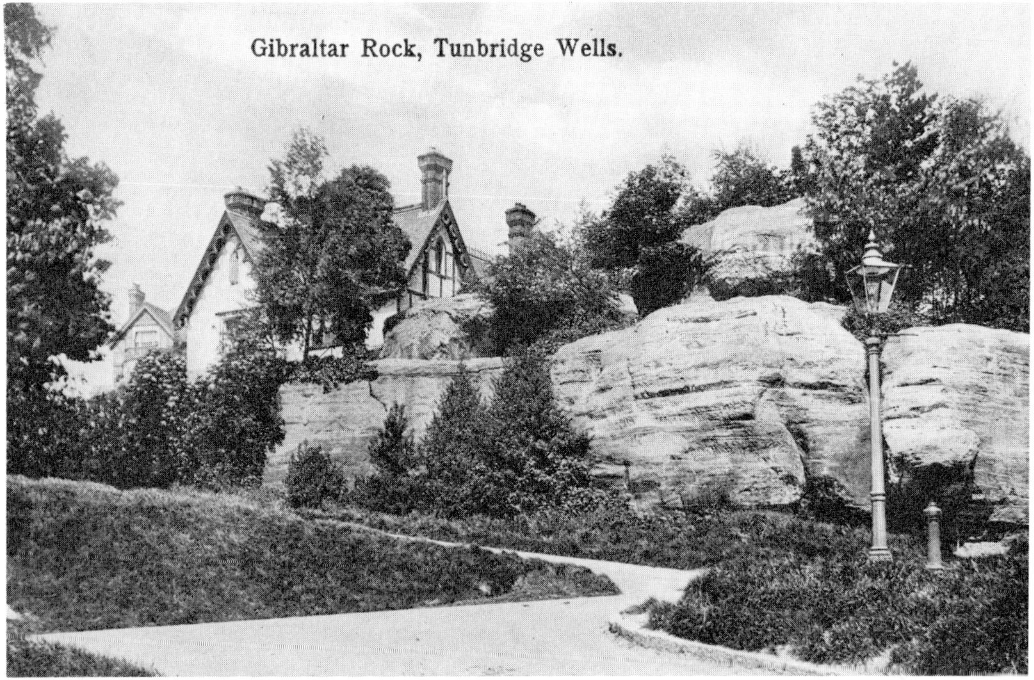

41. The various picturesque cottages nestling amongst the sandstone outcrops on the Common and glimpsed from different angles through the trees have intrigued and confused visitors and inhabitants alike. Which is which, they wonder, being more familiar with the names than their appearance. First in the apex between Mount Ephraim and the London Road is Belleville (see previous postcard), its stuccoed walls no longer half-timbered. Next comes St. Helena Cottage, frequently misnomered as on this Edwardian card; and last of the group and nearest to Church Road stands Gibraltar Cottage (see next postcard). Changes in this view since the beginning of the century have been subtle. The old street gas lamp has gone; trees now perch precariously on the rocks where shrubs and saplings grew, and recent owners in search of privacy have constructed a wall and gate where previously the garden merged into the Common.

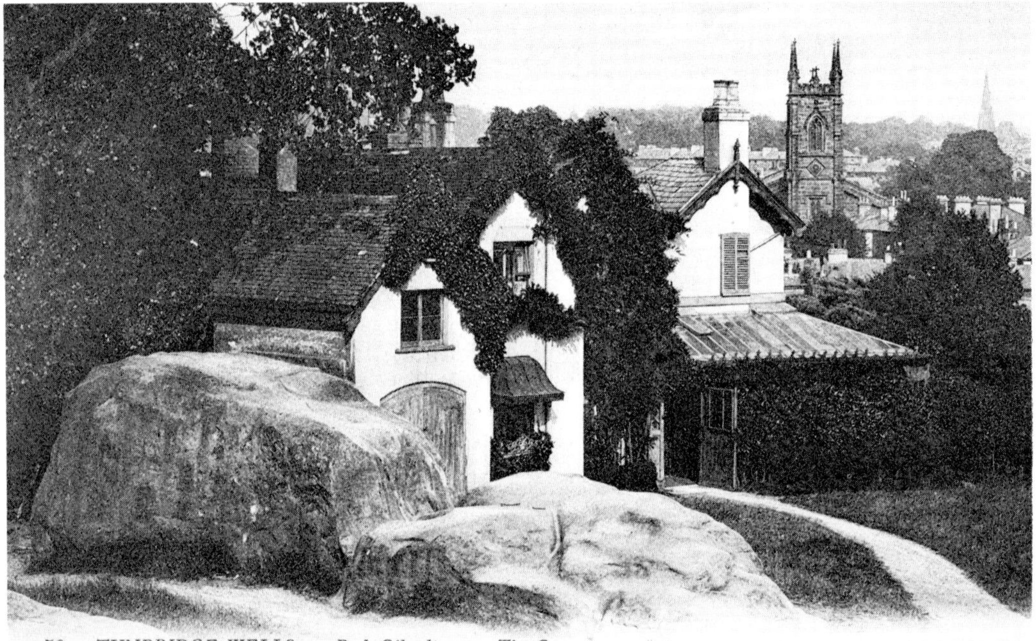

50 TUNBRIDGE WELLS. — Rock Gibraltar. — The Common.

42. Such was its state of delapidation some years back, that Gibraltar Cottage came under threat of demolition; fortunately it was rescued from this fate and repaired, undergoing minor alterations. The coach house entrance was bricked up and a window inset; the canopy of the adjacent window, the glass roofed loggia and shutters above were removed and a modest porch constructed. Until the 1960's it was still possible to look across the town from the hillside above Gibraltar Cottage and see Holy Trinity Church towering like a cathedral above the surrounding houses. Now only the top of the tower with its four pinnacles are visible behind the massive block of Telephone House (see No. 39).

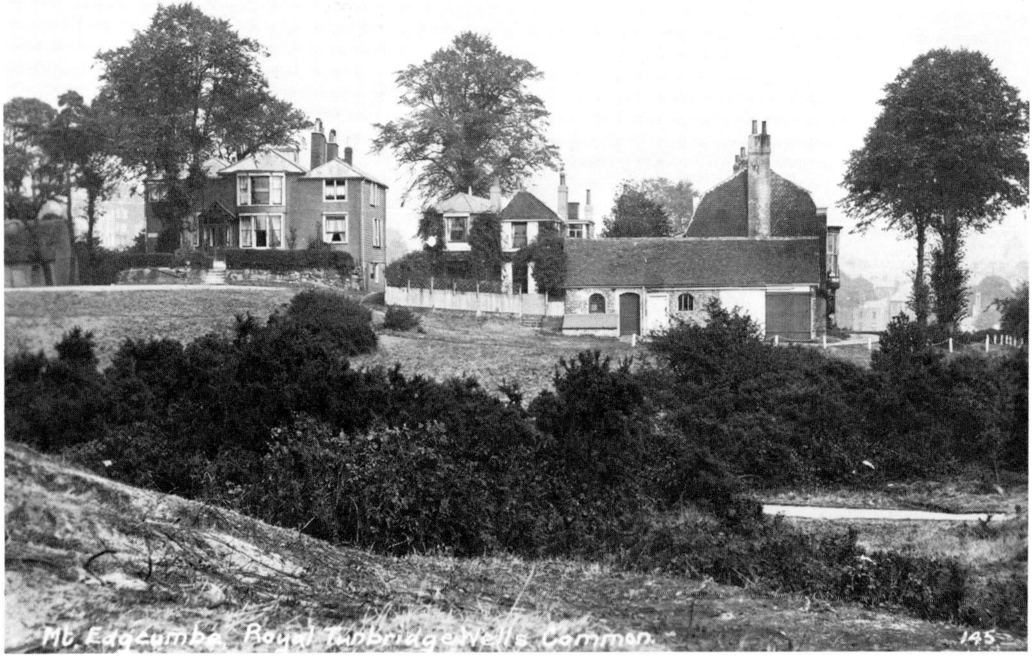

43. Woodlands develop slowly; the change from year to year is scarcely noticeable but half a century can make a vast difference to the landscape. As long as sheep regularly grazed on the Common, only the gorse and deliberate plantings of trees flourished; but when the sheep no longer controlled the young seedlings, birch and oak started to encroach on the former heathland. This distant view of Mount Edgecumbe House and Cottage is now obscured by the woodland that has grown up in the last decades. In recent years the low carriage- and outhouse on the left has been partially demolished to allow modification to the chimney flue and an extra window to be inserted in the main part of the house, and the remaining section converted into garages.

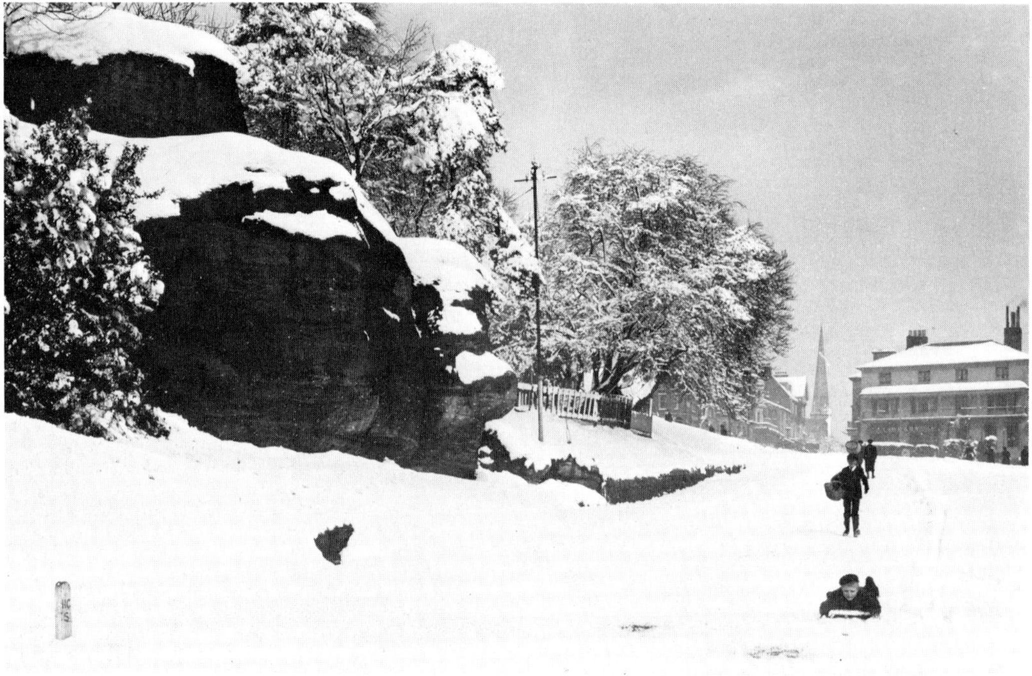

44. *Even in winter, when the snow mantles thick upon the green-sward and prohibits walking to any extent, the undulations of the Common make excellent tracks for tobogganing a sport that youths and maidens indulge in, in ever increasing numbers,* wrote the author of a local guide in 1897. At the beginning of the twentieth century a child might toboggan and an errand boy with basket balanced on head might stride down the centre of what is now the main 'A' road through Tunbridge Wells without fear of traffic. Such motor vehicles as used the roads between 1896 and 1903 travelled at no more than twelve miles per hour, a limit then raised to twenty miles per hour. Opposite the head of the London Road, Oldenburgh House, then the Library of Daniel Williams bookseller and stationer, remains virtually unchanged apart from the first floor balcony; but the neo-gothic spire of Emmanuel Church has since disappeared (see next card).

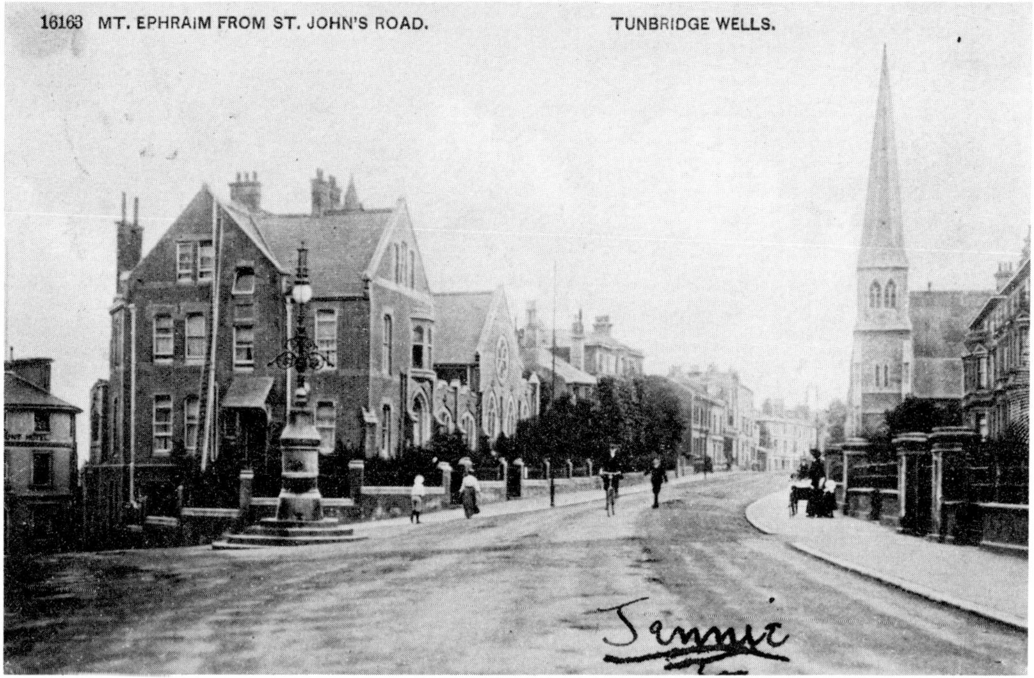

45. For over a century the gothic spire of Emmanuel Church dominated Mount Ephraim. Built to replace the original chapel of the Countess of Huntingdon's Connexion and completed in 1867, it was demolished in 1974 to provide access to a car park at the Kent and Sussex Hospital. In 1897 the non-conformist congregation was divided when the Minister, Reverend James Mountain, took conscientious objection to infant baptism. As the articles of the Countess of Huntingdon's Trust did not permit adult baptism, he decided with considerable local support to establish a rival church. Designed by H.M. Caley (later Mayor of Tunbridge Wells), St. John's Free Church opened for public worship directly opposite the parent church on 2nd October 1901. In the 1940's the premises were transferred to the Presbyterians and renamed St. Andrew's. The magnificent lamp standard and fountain at the road junction have long since disappeared.

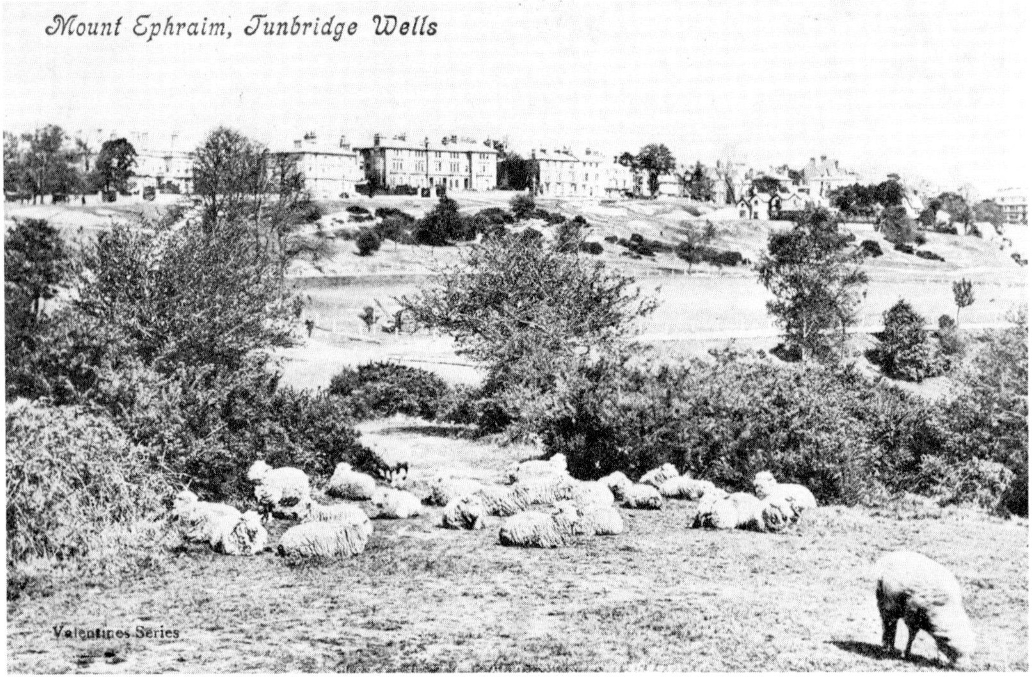

46. *It is with us a prime article of topographic faith, that there is no place like Tunbridge Wells Common,* wrote the author of a local guide in 1880. *Here a flock of South Down sheep are silently grazing beneath the care of an old weather-beaten shepherd, there a merry party of well-mounted youths and maidens are cantering up a turfy slope. In the Spring, large patches of this heath are golden and fragrant with the blossoms of the prickly furze. All summer long the brake tosses its branchy fronds to glimmer in the sun. Here and there patches of camomile yield their aromatic perfume to the breeze. Beneath a noble clump of fir-trees 'an ancient mariner' is scanning with his telescope the rugged sides of Crowborough; down below the broken rocks a party of children are digging in the white glistening sand.* Children still play round the rocks, but gone are the sheep, and gone too is much of the gorse and bracken, engulfed by trees.

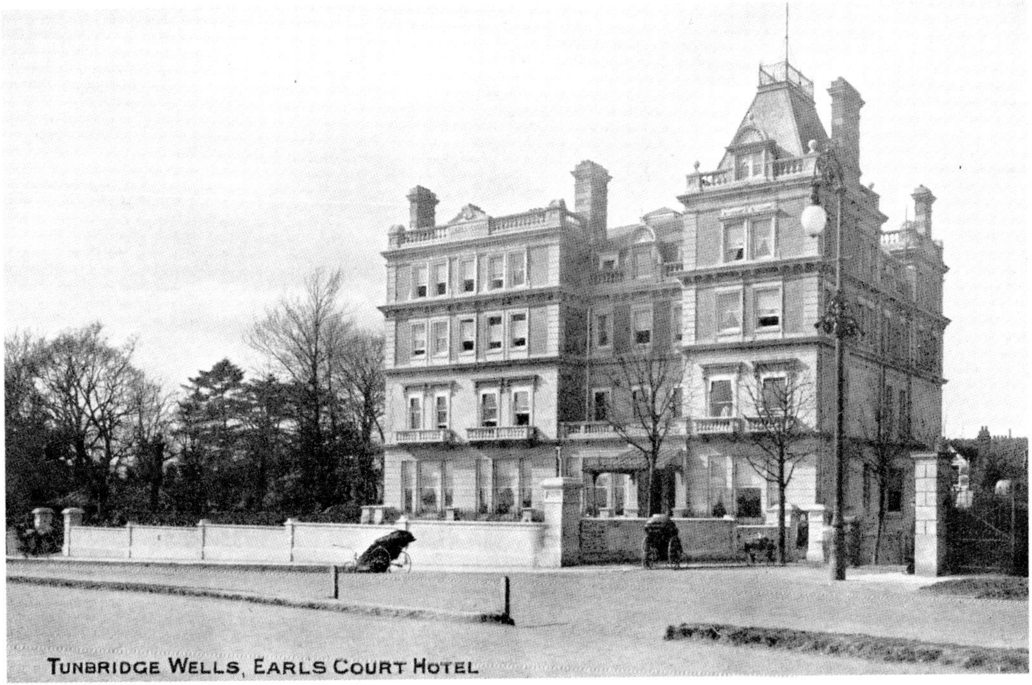

47. The previous view of Mount Ephraim from the Common, photographed at the turn of the century, shows on the skyline to the left, Earl's Court before its conversion into a hotel and the addition of three upper storeys. In 1866, having pulled down an earlier house on the site, the Honourable F.G. Molyneux erected a new residence naming it in honour of his father the Earl of Sefton. After his death the house was first let out in apartments, then in 1901 purchased and after considerable alterations opened as a hotel in 1904. Since then only minor alterations have been made to the exterior. The glass porch was removed and the inscription 'Earls Court Hotel', that proclaimed itself in large capitals along the roof balustrade in the 1930's, was replaced by an equally bold 'Reliance House' when the building became Insurance offices. This in turn was replaced by a less conspicuous inscription at the request of conservationists.

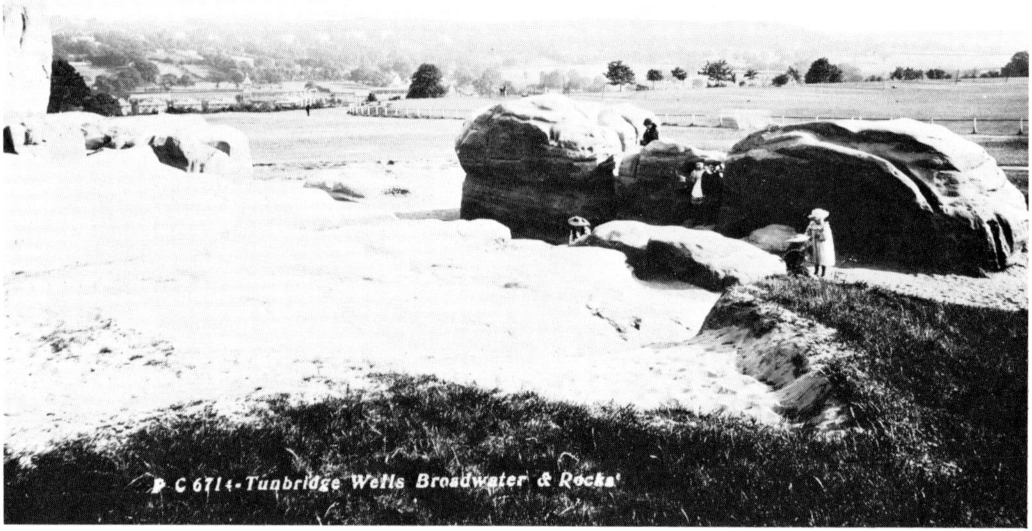

48. *The Cricket Ground on the Common below Mount Ephraim, is admirably suited to this manly game; and is a spot commanding charming views of the country around,* wrote one nineteenth century Guide, *Practice is going on here every day during the season and no week passes which does not yield one or more good matches to the lovers of cricket.* In 1875 it witnessed the famous match between the North and South of England arranged by the Association for Promoting the Interests of the Town, in which three leading batsmen of the South were out for ducks in the first over. The famous W.G. Grace was caught at point from the very first ball delivered, O. Charlwood clean bowled with the second and after playing one ball, G.F. Grace, the champion's youngest brother, was caught off the next at mid off. The game was over in two days instead of the scheduled three, the North winning by one innings and 58 runs.

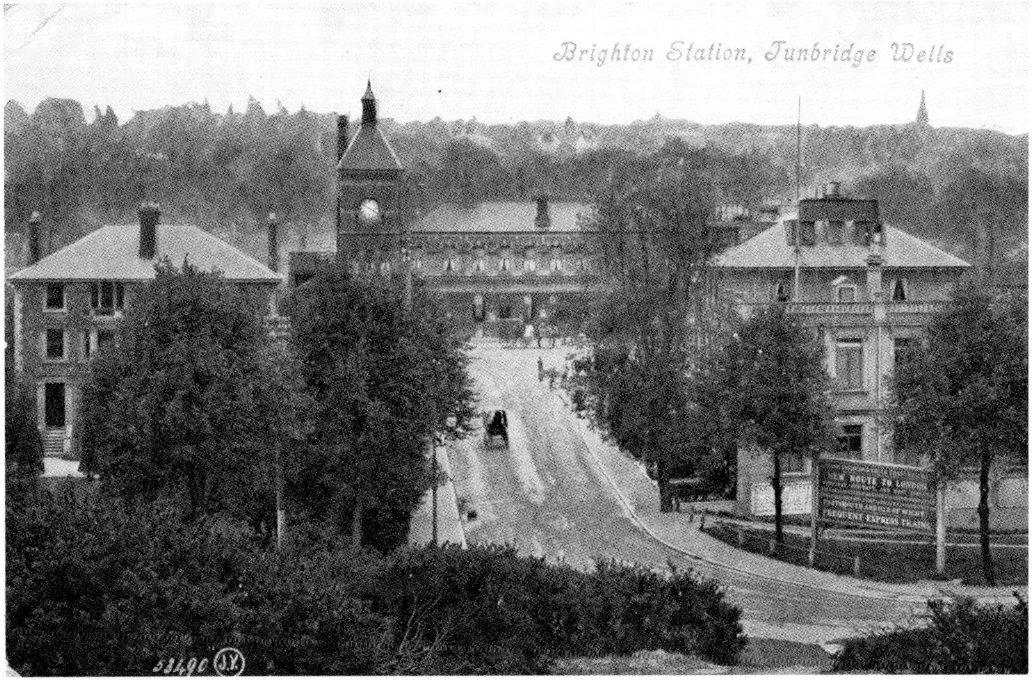

49. At the beginning of the century from the Upper Cricket Ground and Wellington Rocks, as views of the surrounding countryside had not yet been obscured by trees, it was still possible to see the buildings on the far side of Eridge Road, including Tunbridge Wells West Station (see previous picture). The train service had reached the town in the autumn of 1845, terminating at a temporary station on the site of the present Goods Depot and a year later the Central Station was brought into use. On 1st October 1866 the London, Brighton and South Coast Railway extended to Tunbridge Wells from the East Grinstead direction, and the Brighton Station, later renamed the West Station, was constructed. This postcard shows the station as it was in about 1905. Now the passenger service is threatened with closure and the future of the building remains uncertain.

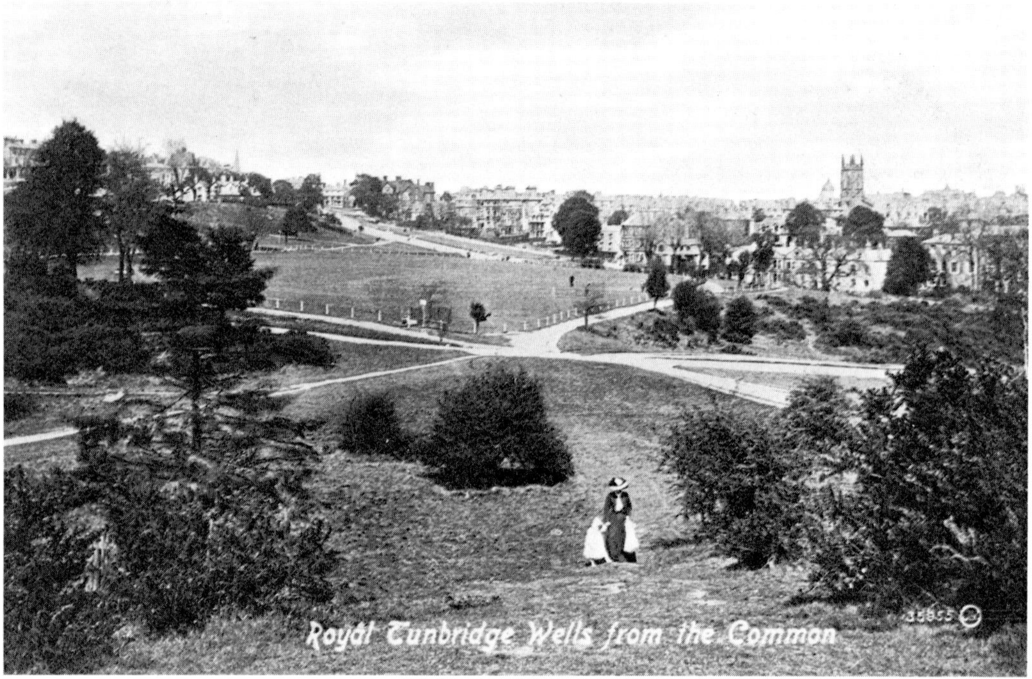

50. From the end of the eighteenth century onwards cricket matches were regularly held on the Upper Cricket Ground, then known as the Racecourse (see No. 48 centre right). To cater for the increased number of fixtures by various clubs using the Common, a new area was levelled in 1885 but the Lower Cricket Ground proved no more satisfactory for high class cricket than the Upper. Players complained that the wicket was ruined by grazing sheep and cattle, as well as being trampled by the public. Consequently, in 1895 the Tunbridge Wells Cricket, Football and Athletic Club was formed with the purpose of promoting those sports and acquiring suitable land on which to play; a year later work began on the Nevill Ground. Although the Lower Cricket Ground (centre of picture) has survived as an open sports field, since this Edwardian photograph was taken tree planting has transformed the surrounding area of the Common.

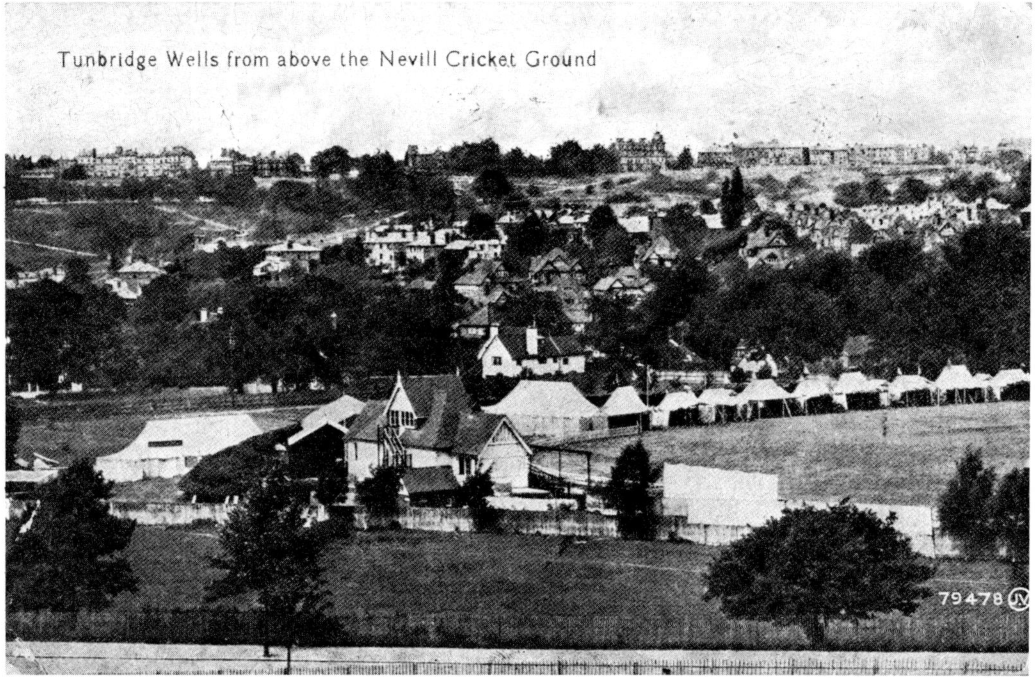

51. Traditionally cricket had always been played on the Common, but in 1890 in response to constant complaints about the state of the pitch, the Tradesmen's Association suggested the development of a new ground, though neither of the proposed sites in St. John's Road and Camden Park proved feasible. In 1896, a year after the Tunbridge Wells Cricket, Football and Athletic Club was founded, work began on a site in Cumberland Walk leased from the Marquess of Abergavenny, after whom it was named the Nevill Ground. Opened by the Marquess on Whit Monday 1898, it became the headquarters of the Tunbridge Wells Cricket Club and the Bluemantle's as well as the local Hockey and Lawn Tennis Clubs. The original pavilion built by the local firm Strange & Sons was burnt down by militant Suffragettes as a bastion of male privilege, only to rise within nine weeks like a phoenix from the ashes. This view shows the pavilion in about 1925.

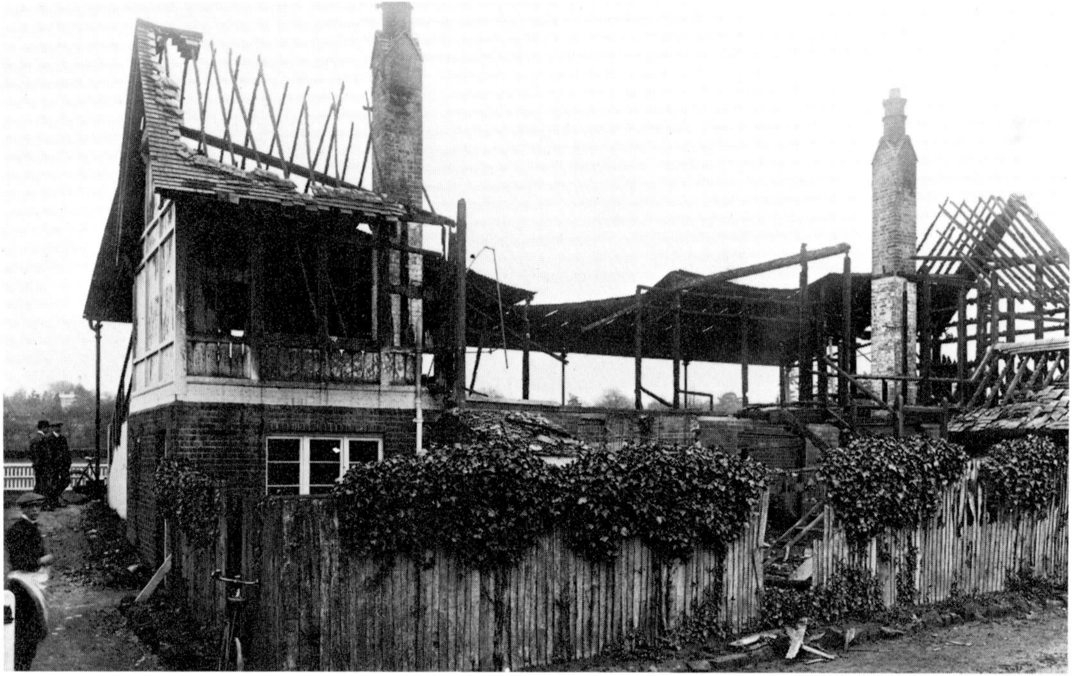

52. 'Sir A. Conan Doyle on Malicious Monkey Tricks' read a headline referring to the protest meeting in the Great Hall following the burning of the Nevill Pavilion on 11th April 1913. No one doubted that it was the work of militant Suffragettes, for *Not alone the discovery of Mrs. Pankhurst's photograph pinned on the grass before the wreck of the Pavilion, not the Suffragist 'literature' which had been scattered around, but the senseless character of the crime stamps it as one of the series of acts of these wild women.* Suffragettes among the crowd unable to obtain admission to the Hall were *booed and severely hustled. Their placards were torn from them, and their literature scattered all over the place. Eggs in a somewhat advanced state of decadence were thrown at the ladies and some of them found their mark.* A new Pavilion was completed within hours of start of play in the Cricket Week match against Worcestershire.

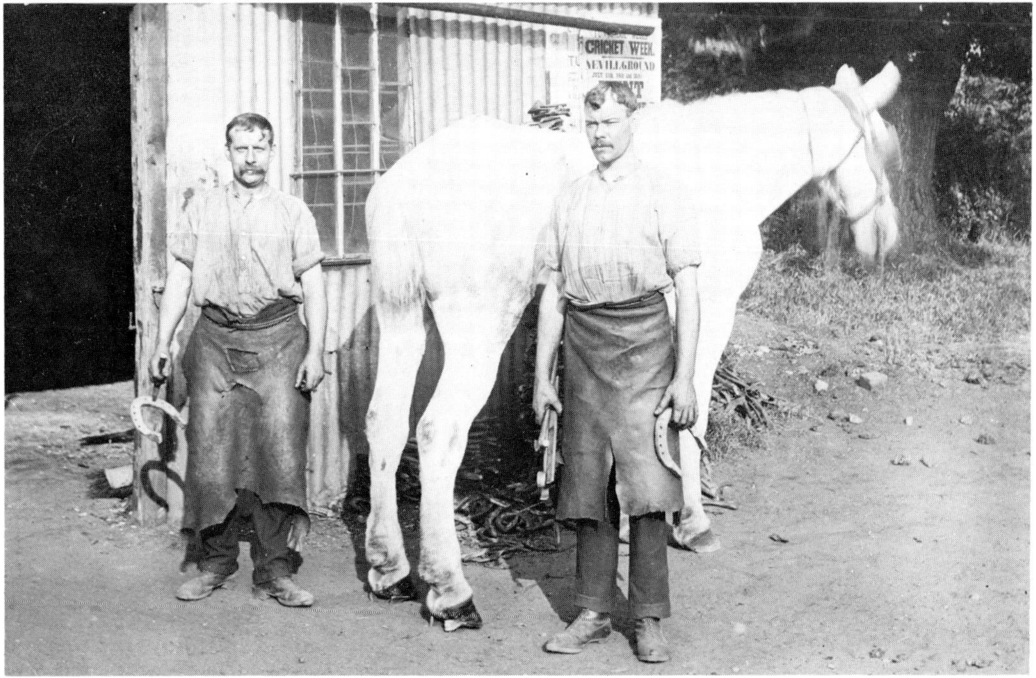

53. This rare postcard portrays farriers outside a local forge onto whose corrugated wall is attached a sporting poster advertising the Tunbridge Wells Cricket Week at the Nevill Ground on July 13th-15th. County cricket had been played on Tunbridge Wells Common intermittently between 1845 and 1884, with frequent complaints as to the appalling condition of the Race course (Upper Cricket Ground). With the opening of the Nevill Ground county cricket was encouraged to return to the town, the first Championship match being held in 1901. Teams from the adjacent county were frequent visitors. The poster on the forge seems to refer to the Kent versus Sussex match of 1911.

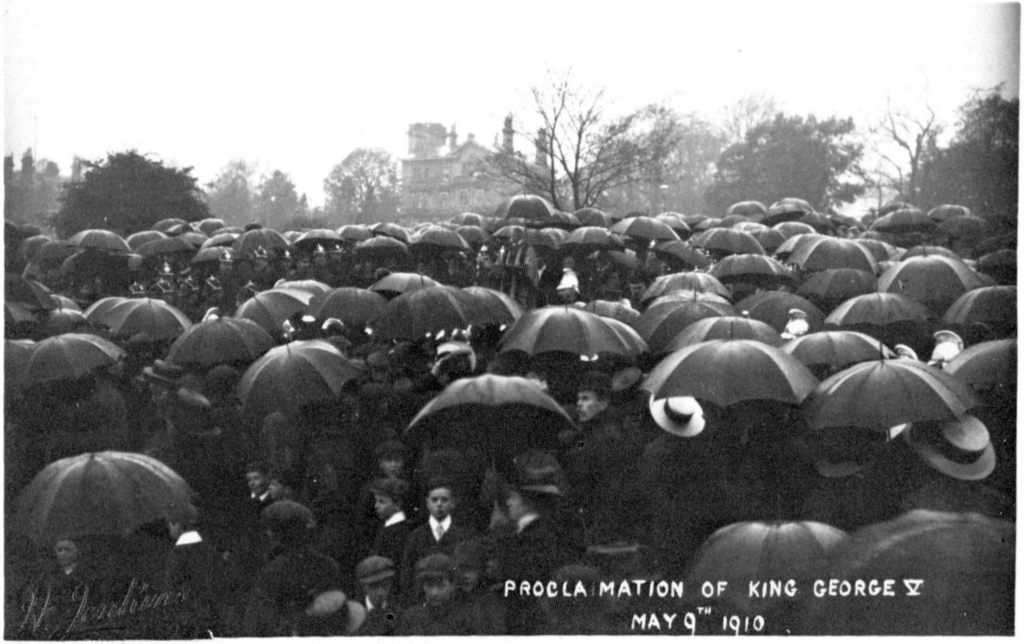

54. Public rejoicing at the accession of a new monarch was subdued at the proclamation of George V for the public had not recovered from the shock caused by the death of Edward VII. Newspapers had announced that throughout the county the historic event would take place at nine o'clock on the Monday morning, but at Tunbridge Wells it was not possible until the afternoon. In heavy rain, a sombre crowd heard the proclamation read by the Deputy Mayor from a small platform draped in crepe and purple outside the Town Hall. The Union Flag was raised, three cheers called for His Majesty, and the National Anthem sung. *A move was then made to the Common, the members of Council walking in procession behind a body of police and firemen. Standing on a seat at the Lower Cricket Ground, Alderman Caley again read the curiously worded notice to an even larger crowd, cheers being raised for the King and the National Anthem sung as before.*

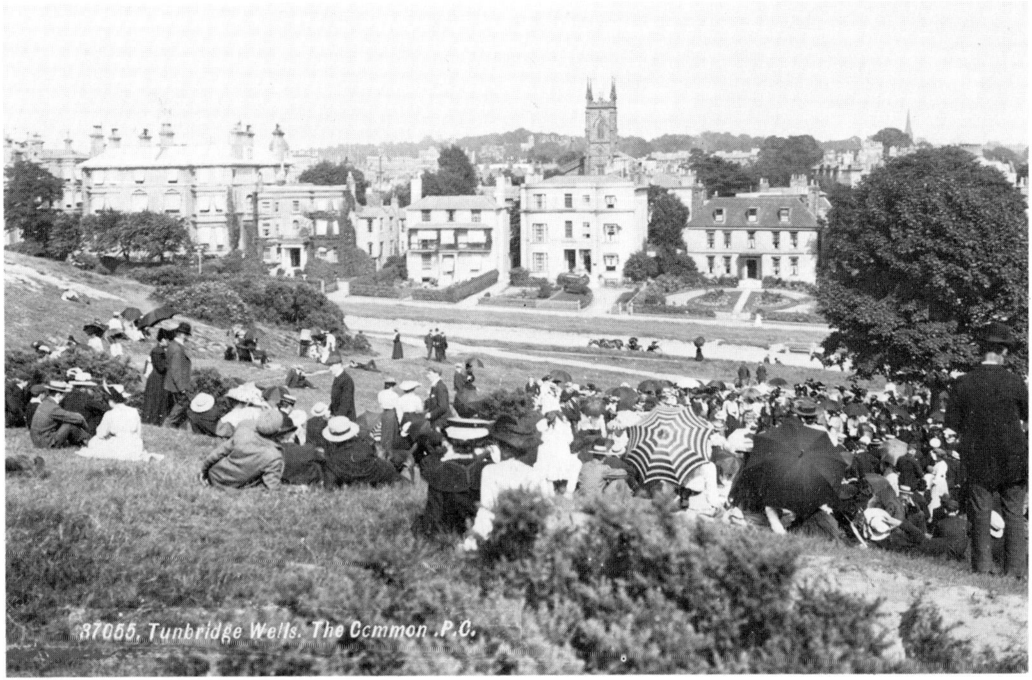

55. Edwardian postcards such as this were often captioned 'Sunday afternoon on the Common', giving truth to the saying 'What the ocean is to a sea-bathing town, that the Common is to Tunbridge Wells'. During the First World War, the Common witnessed a strange transformation when an advance guard of Territorial Royal Engineers from Birmingham assisted by a corps of local Boy Scouts pitched tents and got everything shipshape for the main force, which arrived on 10th September 1914 and encamped on the Lower Cricket Ground to await further orders. Everything was catered for, including a recreation tent outside the encampment proper, 'well furnished for reading, writing, and games, while a piano was also provided'. Great was the excitement among the ladies and the local youth, intrigued also at the laying of a field telegraph line through the gorse bushes. The novelty of the occasion was celebrated in a series of postcards (see next picture).

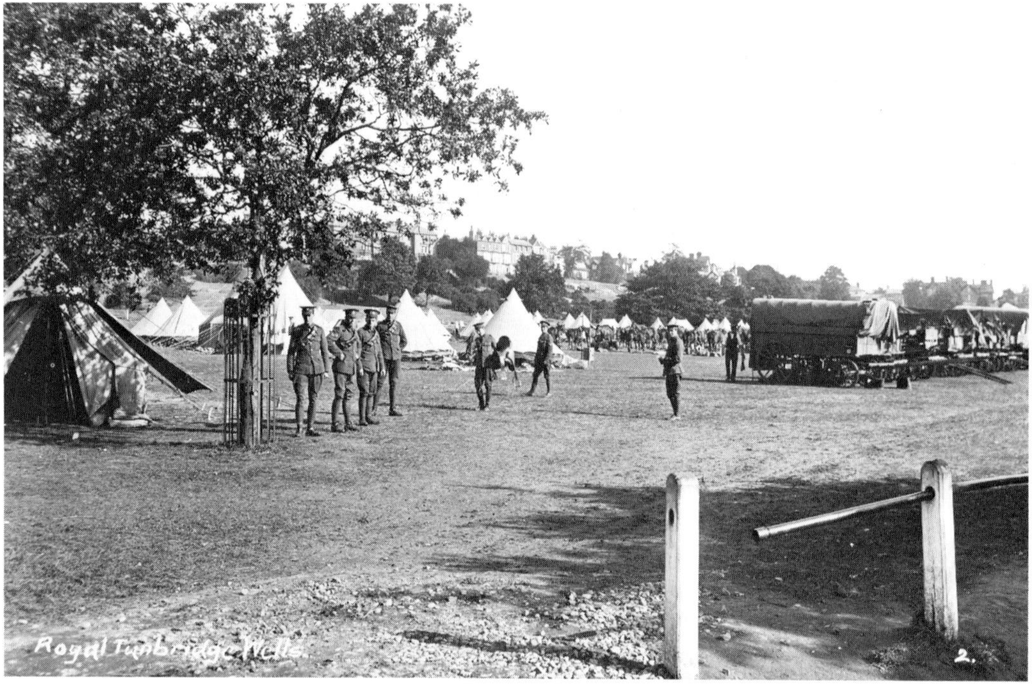

56. Under the headline 'Sunday afternoon on the Common. A Contrast', a journalist described the military encampment in September 1914 as *a great centre of feminine interest on Sunday afternoon. The rows of beautiful horses tethered to the railings or being exercised were unfailing objects of admiration, and many ladies brought with them baskets of apples to feed the horses, which appeared to particularly appreciate the delicacy. The bell-tents, with a distant glimpse of their interiors, and the field kitchen were also subjects of interested curiosity to townsfolk, who, living far from a garrison town, have never had the military quartered in their midst, and who find this unfamiliar sight a most interesting one. The cooking of rations and the boiling of big cauldrons of tea over a wood-fire afforded endless interest, and the tea tables, laden with plentiful supplies of lettuce and jam, came in for much interest.*

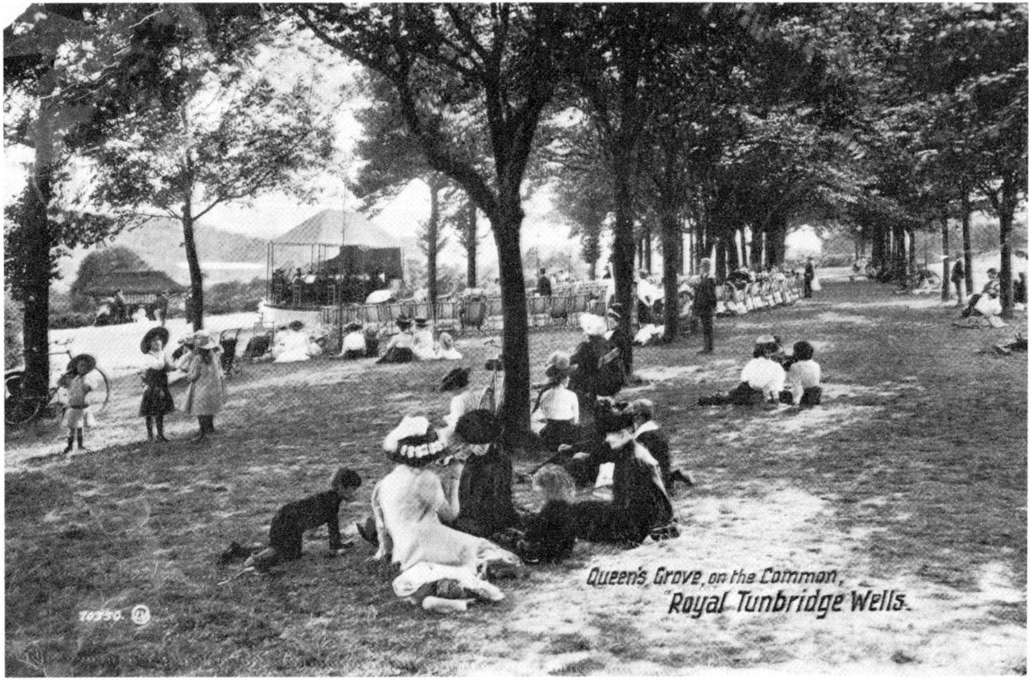

57. The original Queen's Grove, a triple row of birch trees, was planted by the inhabitants of Tunbridge Wells as a 'monument of gratitude to their royal and generous benefactress' Princess Anne on her accession in 1702. With time the trees decayed and a number were replaced but although their appearance by then was 'not the most flourishing', it was decided to emulate this sylvan tribute by planting a double avenue of elms, limes and sycamores nearby in 1835 as a 'public testimonial of respect' to commemorate the visits of Princess Victoria and her mother the Duchess of Kent. In Edwardian times, the Royal Victoria Grove (frequently, as here, miscalled the Queen's Grove) was a favourite resort on summer days, 'a lovely shady retreat on the Common's brow from which wide panoramic views' could be obtained. The views are now obscured by oak, birch and bramble; the bandstand's foundations lie buried beneath the undergrowth.

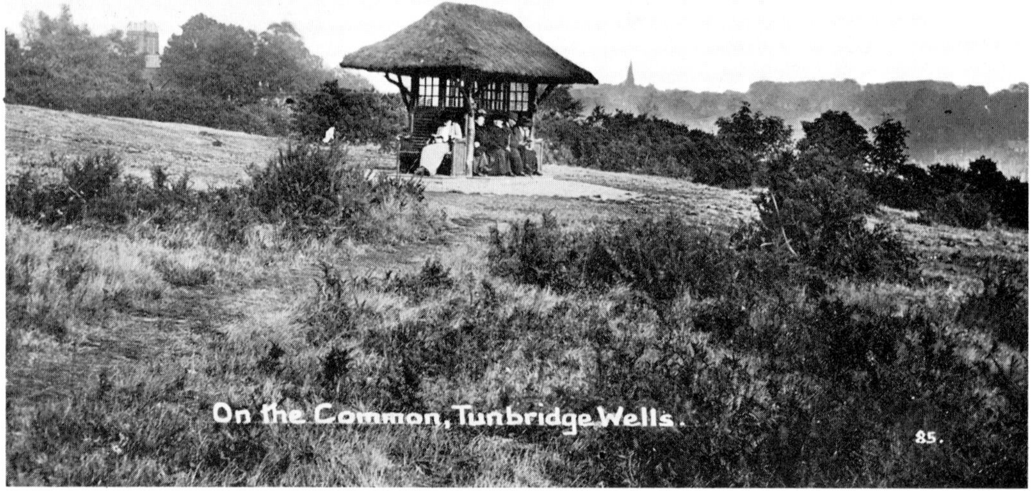

58. Reporting to the Tradesmen's Association in June 1907, one worthy remarked *there was hardly a month passed but what visitors had enquired why covered seats were not placed on the Common... with gratification... he now heard that they (the Conservators) had decided to place one seat which might lead to more... later. He would suggest that they should be shut up at night to give confidence to those who were perhaps a little suspicious as to their use.* Visitors and inhabitants were appreciative; one even waxed poetical: *Helter, skelter, here's a pelter, / Run away and find the Shelter; / My hat is spoilt, my shoes wet thro', / Run hard and fast, what shall we do? / Oh, that the Shelter was more handy / On asphalt path, not wet and sandy; / But let's be glad, for mercies small, / Curse not, for fear the Shelter fall. / On Summer days all hot and blazing, / We'll bless the folks for Shelter raising; / And pray the gods may see their way / To put up more another day.*

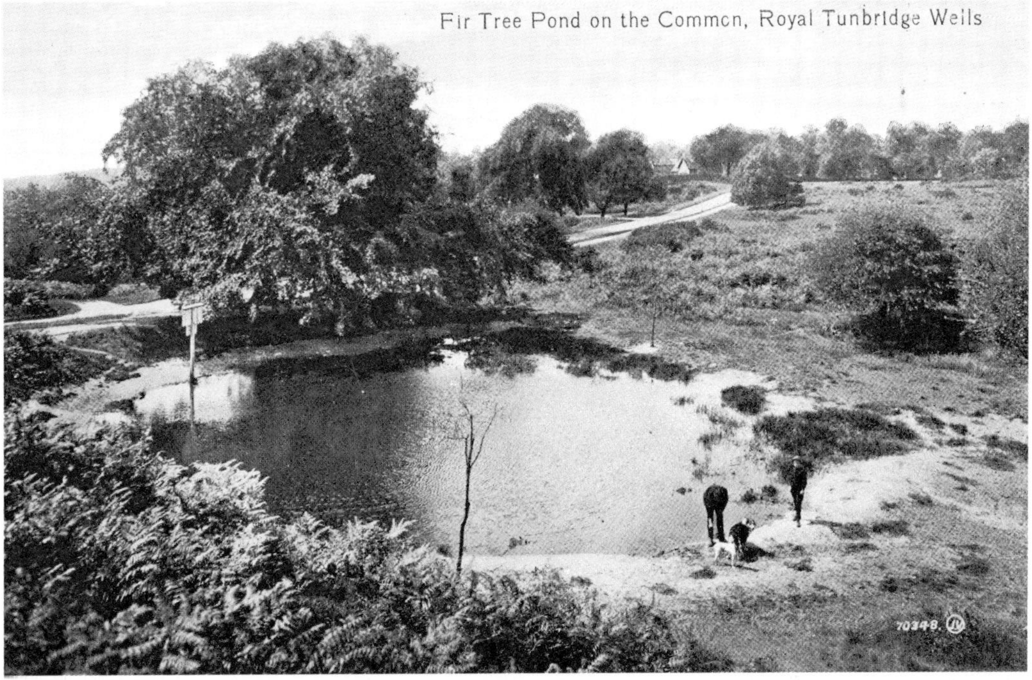

59. Formerly there were some six or seven ponds on the Common, but by the end of the nineteenth century all but two, Brighton Lake and Fir Tree Pond, had been drained or filled in. Continued neglect has led to this part of the Common becoming overgrown with birch, oak and an occasional hawthorn, the young trees flourishing in the pond itself which at certain times is little more than a marshy hollow. The two Scotch firs, known as Darby and Joan, which long dominated the skyline of that part of the Common and gave their name to the pond, are now no more. Three small pines planted on the site continue the tradition, and like their predecessors shade a wooden seat.

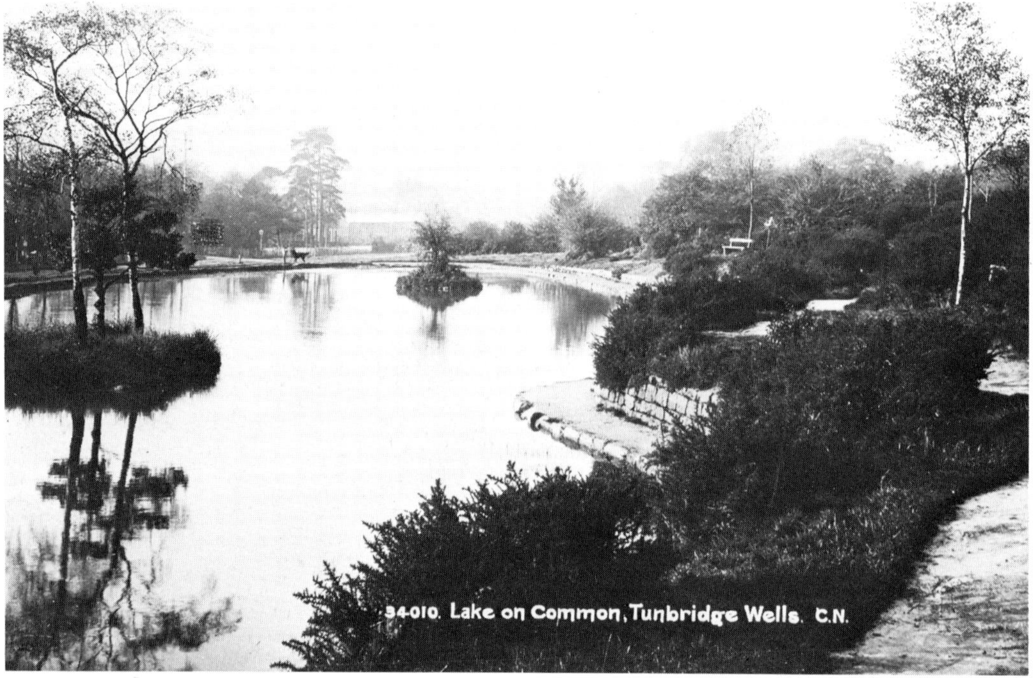

60. *At the present,* wrote a correspondent to the Advertiser in 1897 referring to the Brighton Lake, *the little lake, which at the time of its construction bore the soubriquet of 'Pope's Folly' is not very ornamental and its utility not very great. Although a sign-board on its banks bears an inscription, which time and the weather have almost obliterated, pointing out the liability which anyone incurs by throwing stones or missiles into it, or otherwise destroying the pond, yet the warning is more honoured in the breach than the observance, and daily it is made the washing tub for all sorts and conditions of dogs, whose owners find it a capital place for exercising and bathing their animals.* A contemporary who could recall the excavation of the lake found this part of the Common still quite charming *especially since the Conservators have improved it by planting trees, putting some seats and a walk round the pond.*

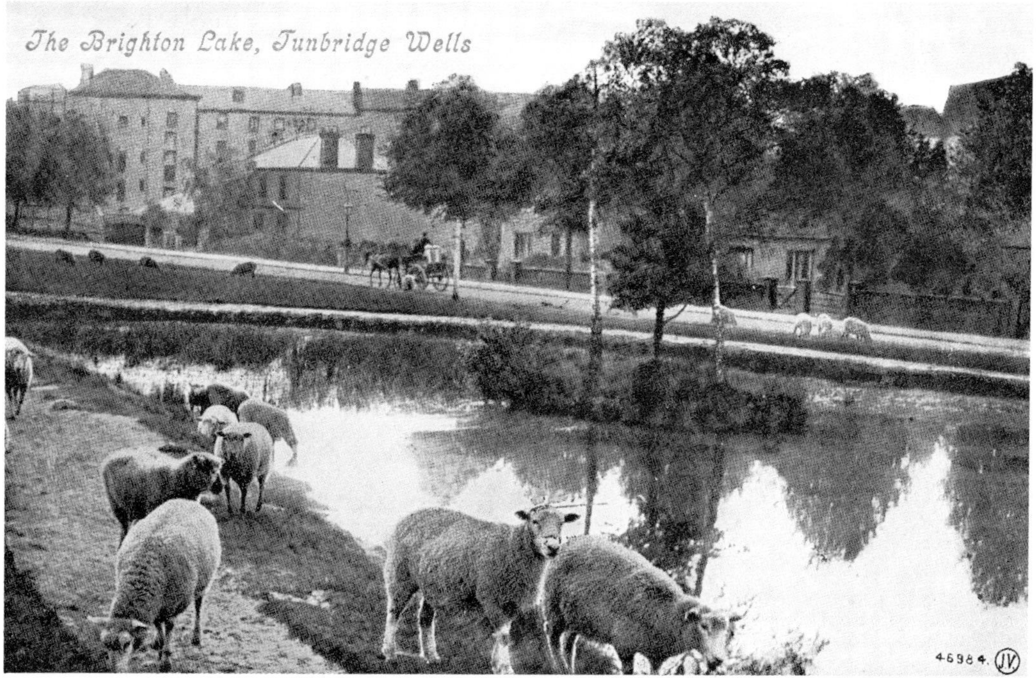

61. Since this postcard view appeared as an illustration in the Official Guide of 1903, trees and undergrowth have encroached, practically obliterating the terrace walk. In the middle of the last century the pond was little more than a bog until, following a severe winter, the Reverend W.L. Pope raised funds in 1858 to provide work for the town's unemployed. One of the improvement projects was the creation out of the existing morass of Brighton Lake, disparagingly known as 'Pope's Puddle'. Intended as a place for children to play, the banks were equipped with long hooked poles 'wherewith to secure a firm purchase on the nether garments of any small boy who might happen to fall in'. Years later the poles turned up again, stored beneath the roof of King Charles Church and were converted into flag poles. A garage now occupies the site of Roseberry and Richmond Lodge (centre) which were demolished in the late sixties.

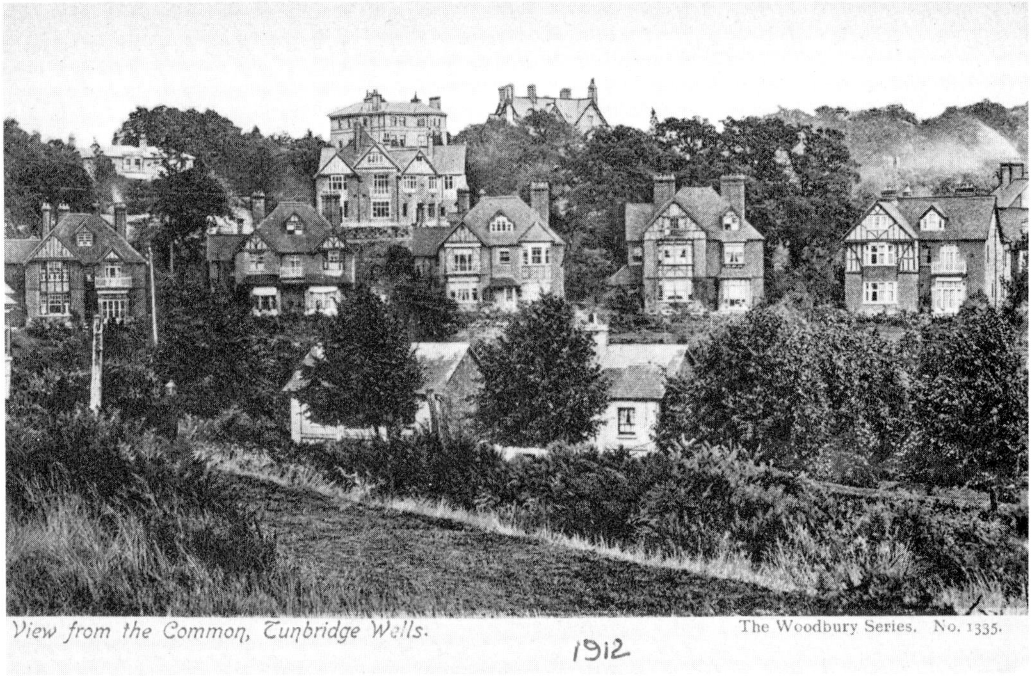

62. This view, dating from 1912, is scarcely recognisable although all the houses in the middle ground and distance still exist. Against the skyline are Nos. 10 to 14 Frant Road, known then as Sussex Rise, Beverley and Eversley; and across the middle distance are Nos. 1 to 5 Linden Park, then called Braidswood, Marlborough, Linden Lodge, Doon Brae and Oakdene. The cottages in front, partly hidden by trees, were on the Eridge Road between the Pump Room and Montacute Gardens, and survived until the early sixties when they were pulled down prior to the building of the Union Square shopping precinct. The old view is not only hidden by the new buildings, but by the dense woodland that now grows on this part of the Common.

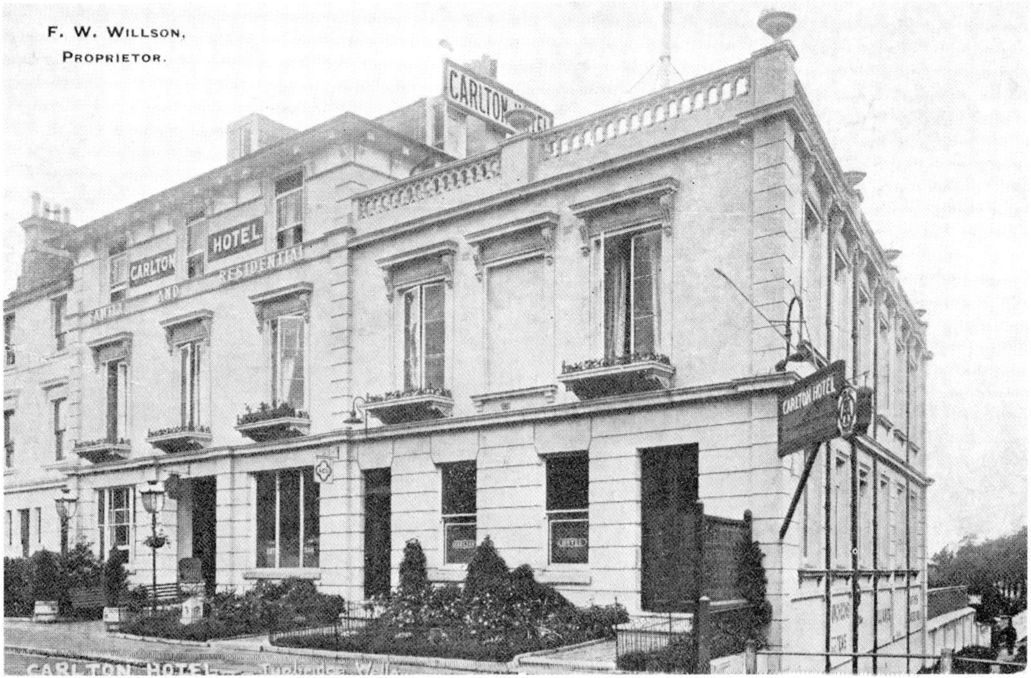

63. Constructed as a private residence, the Carlton was converted into a hotel to cater for travellers arriving at the Brighton Station by the 'New Route to London' in the 1880's. During the brief period of the Municipal Telephonic System (1901-1903) when the Central Exchange was in Calverley Parade, the Carlton Hotel was one of only four public call offices. About this time, the proprietor advertised it as *For Families and Gentlemen. Facing the Common and close to the London, Brighton and South Coast Railway. Billiards – the largest and best ventilated Room in the Town. Bath & Smoking Rooms. Large Dining Room... capable of seating 100. Bedrooms with all the latest up-to-date Improvements. Lighted by Electric Light.* About 1926 another proprietor issued this postcard. In the late thirties, the Carlton was renamed the Lord Cornwallis Inn; later the side wing received alterations and a front extension to the Bar.

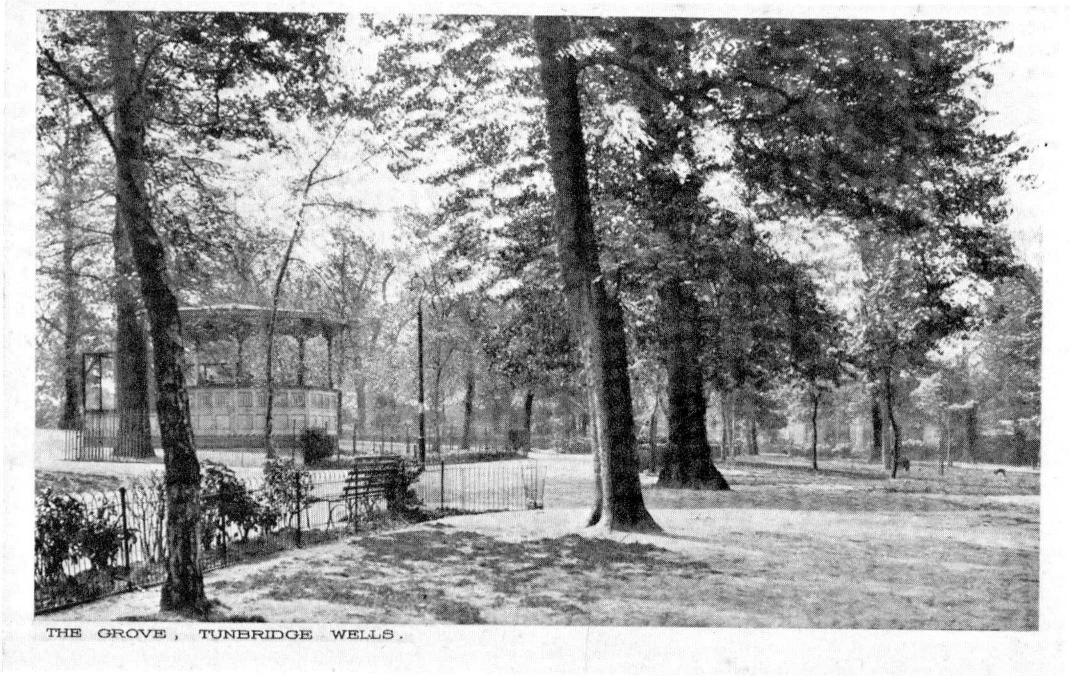

64. In 1896 the Town Surveyor was instructed by the Railway and Parks Committee to prepare plans for a bandstand in Mount Sion Grove, with 'an arrangement to shelter part of the audience in wet weather', though it was feared that the available funds would not be sufficient for the purpose. Opportunely a secondhand bandstand came onto the market the following spring, originally designed for Warrior Square, St. Leonards, but removed because of complaints by tenants and property owners. *But for the recent gales the stand would have been practically as good as new; however, it was seen and purchased after the storm, hence at a considerable reduction from the price first asked; when it is erected, with a new coat of paint (which I believe all outdoor bandstands require annually), I feel sure it will give the burgesses every satisfaction.* And it did for many years, though by the 1930's it had fallen into a deplorable state.

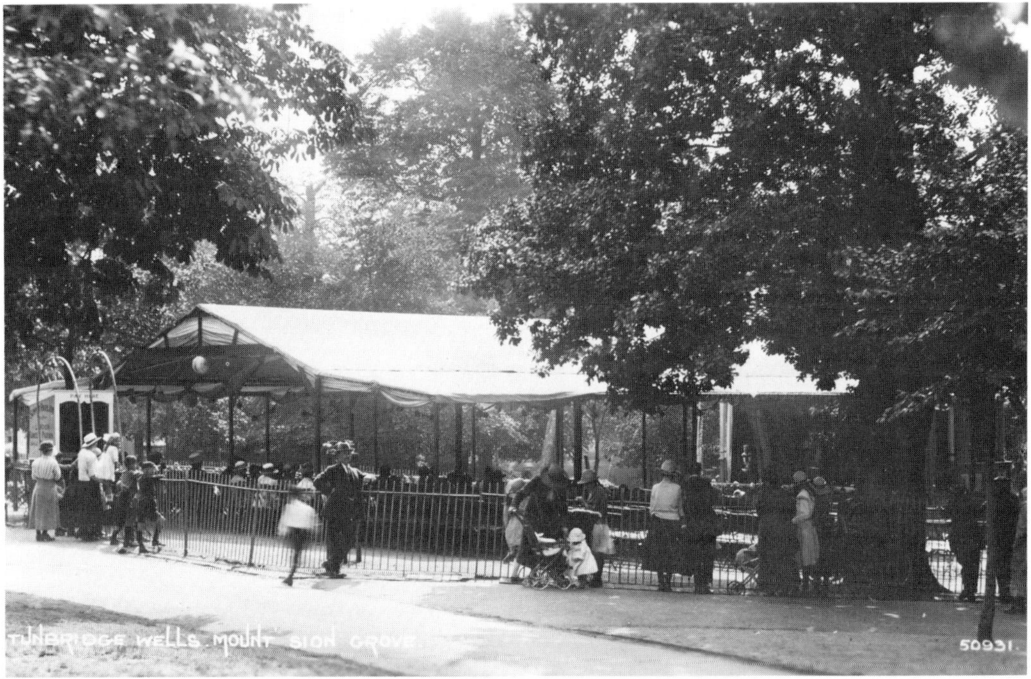

65. For many years between the wars alfresco entertainments were given 'every afternoon and evening by good-class concert parties from May to September'. Almost contemporary with this view came the great hailstorm of May 1922 (see No. 25) when *A most remarkable sight was to be witnessed in Mount Sion Grove. The fury of the storm and the gigantic proportion of the hailstones resulted in vast quantities of chestnut blossoms being forced onto the ground from the overhanging branches. Almost all the paths through the Grove were obliterated and from a distance, the area looked one complete carpet of grass and blossom. A performance was in progress at the Summer Pavilion at the time and thanks to the elaborate arrangements made by the Manager... it was possible to complete the entertainment without any serious difficulty. The audience were well protected, and the awning stood its test well and all underneath were quite dry.*

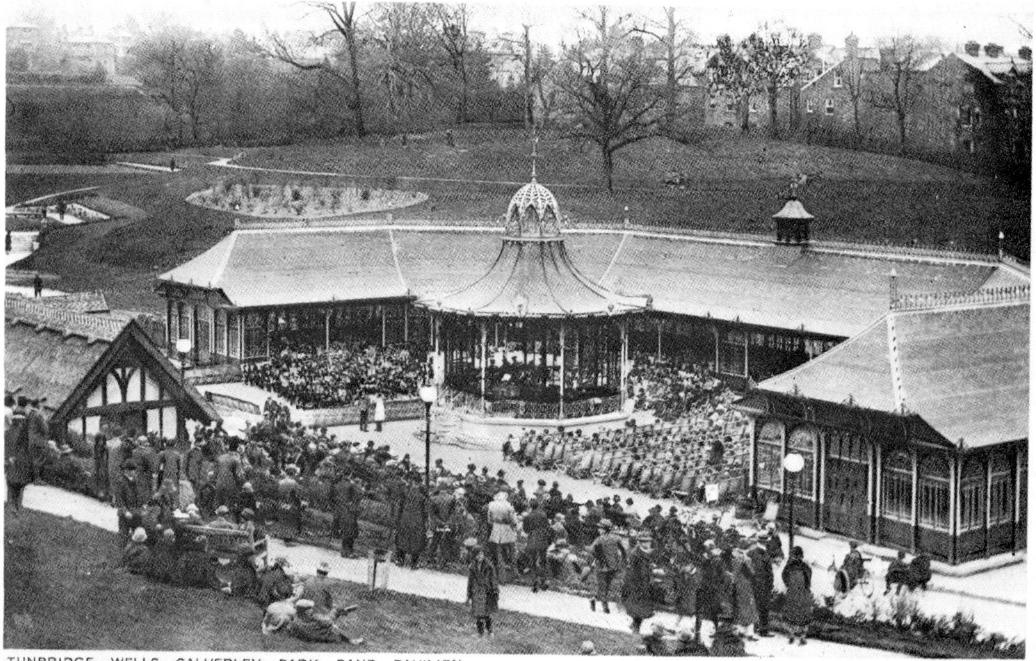

TUNBRIDGE WELLS. CALVERLEY PARK BAND PAVILION 60836.

66. *Nothing is more pleasant on summer evenings than to watch, as the sun dips behind the distant hills, the myriad lights appear and scintillate from the Pavilion and Bandstand* enthused the Official Town Guide. Opened at Easter 1926 with a programme of music by the Band of the Scots Guards, the Pavilion of glass, iron and wood construction with asbestos tiled roof supported by ornamental iron trusses, was intended to provide covered seating for 1,200 spectators and an equal number on the paved area immediately surrounding the Bandstand. When destroyed by a fire-bomb in the summer of 1940, the Pavilion had not been a success being 'cold, draughty and acoustically imperfect' and performances by military bands during the summer months for the most part poorly attended.

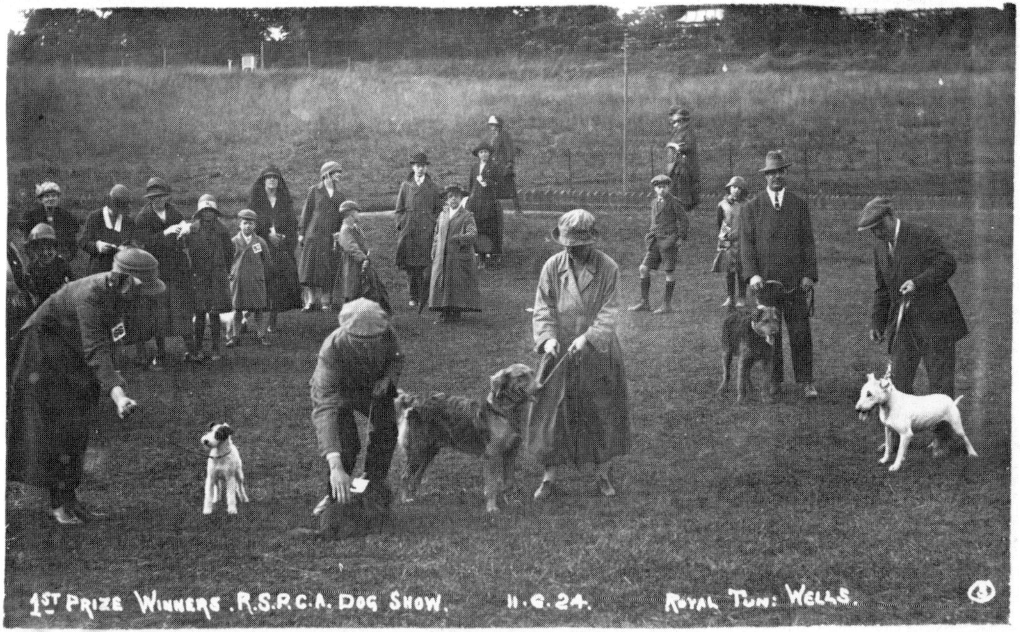

67. As late as 1920 the Corporation acquired fifteen and a half acres of Calverley Park as a public recreation ground at a purchase price of ten thousand pounds. It was immediately provided with tennis courts, bowling and putting greens and a miniature golf course. Walks, terraces and gardens were laid out, including an Italian rose garden whose character, however, was transformed in the thirties by the erection at its centre of an oriental monument. The massive bronze Burmese bell, suspended between carved columns originally surmounted by guardian deities (since vandalised), was presented by a former Mayor of the town Colonel Sladen. The grounds were a popular venue for fêtes, concerts, flower shows and other outdoor events such as the subject of this postcard, the 1924 Dog Show organised by the Royal Society for the Prevention of Cruelty to Animals.

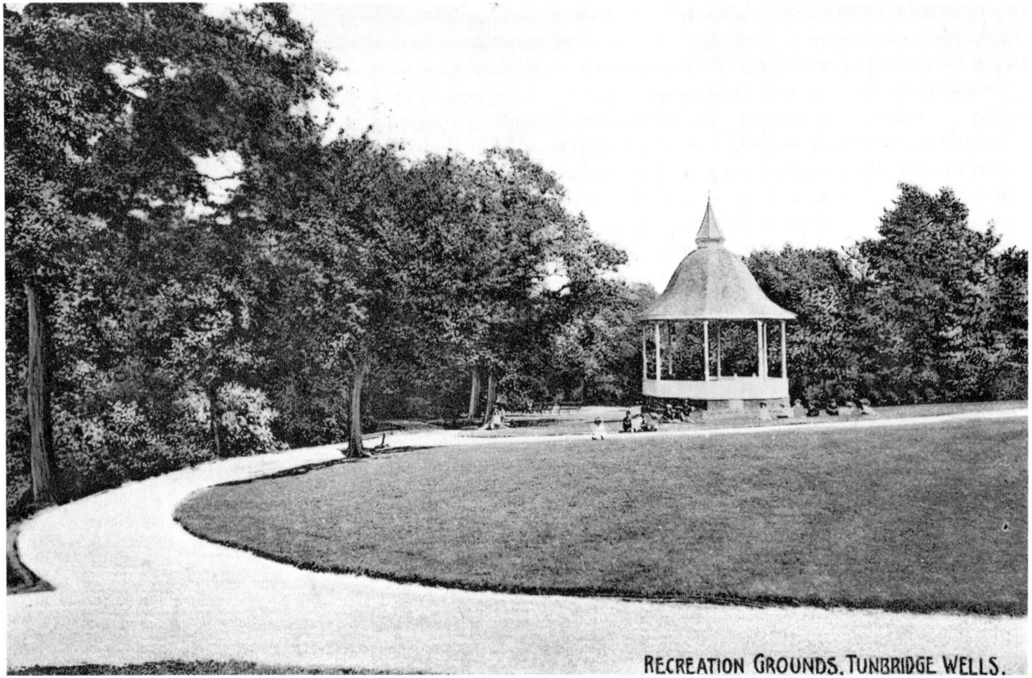

68. The bandstand that once stood above the lakes in the Grosvenor Recreation Ground was presented to the town by Councillor Elvy Robb in memory of his late father. Formally opened by the Mayor on 7th September 1899, it was described as *of an ornamental character, octagonal in shape, and of sufficient dimensions. It was built by Mr. F. Skinner, from a design by Mr. Henry Elwig, junr, who was much complimented on the convenience and appearance of the stand which has a brick base surmounted by a course on which rests a wood panelling with circular mouldings painted in white and blue. Around are eight pitch-pine fluted and moulded columns supporting a bell-shaped tile roof, over which is a lead covered pinnacle with ornamental finish. The stand is lighted by fourlight gaseliers, and let into the brick plinth is a stone with a carved shield on which it is intended to place a memorial inscription.*

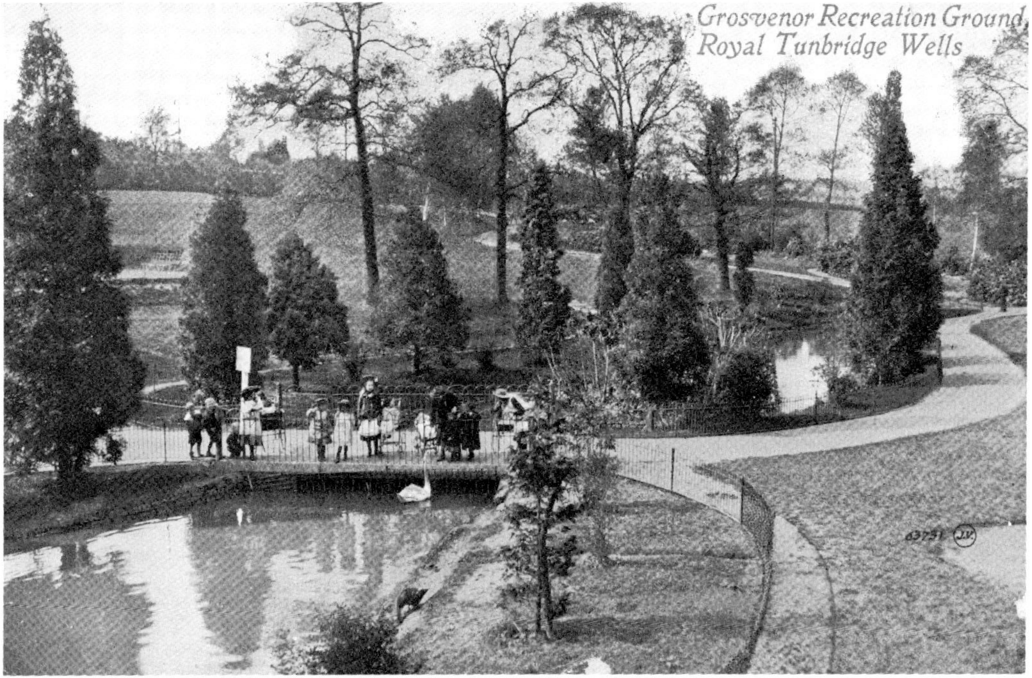

69. When the Corporation bought out the Water Company, four acres of the site of the old waterworks was reserved for a recreation ground, and an additional four acres presented to the town by J. Stone-Wigg, the first Mayor of the Borough. Opened in 1889, it was described in Edwardian guide books as having a large portion *fenced off and laid out in park-like fashion where flowers, waterfalls, well kept paths and borders, seats, and often music enhance the comfort and enjoyment of the visitor. Near at hand is the Town Swimming Bath – the largest in the South of England – where many a doughty water-polo battle is contested during the warm days of summer.* The bandstand, which stood near the present paddling pool (see No. 68), has long since disappeared, the ornamental ponds in the lower part of the grounds seen here were filled in the forties and the ground further levelled more recently. By 1950 the open-air swimming bath had also closed.

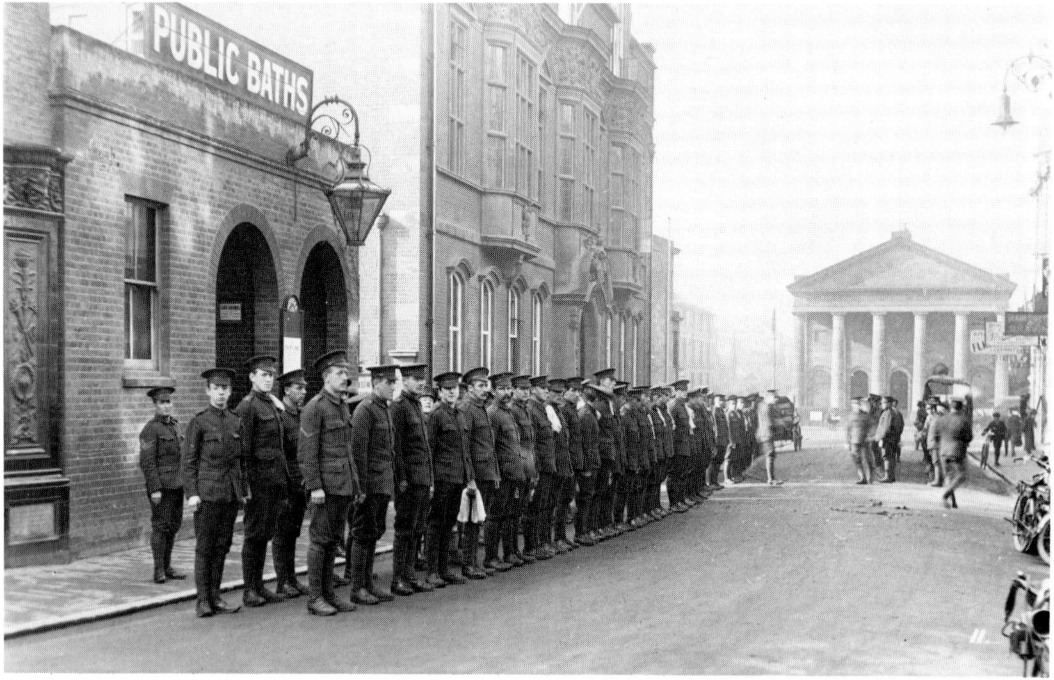

70. The only direct experience of the Great War felt by Tunbridge Wells was when an off-course Zeppelin deposited three bombs in Calverley Park smashing every window in the vicinity. But due to its strategic situation, soldiers from all over England as well as local volunteers gathered to await drafting across to France. Here a corps of territorials are on parade outside the Baths. Opened on 5th October 1898, the first building in the new Civic Centre complex had only a temporary façade on Monson Road, as it was intended ultimately to construct a front to harmonise with that of the Technical Institute next door. However, when the latter was completed in 1902, the idea of refronting the Public Baths was forgotten and never revived. In the 1970's the building was converted into a Sports Hall and more recently into a shop, as has also the former Mount Pleasant Congregational Church with its classical portico.

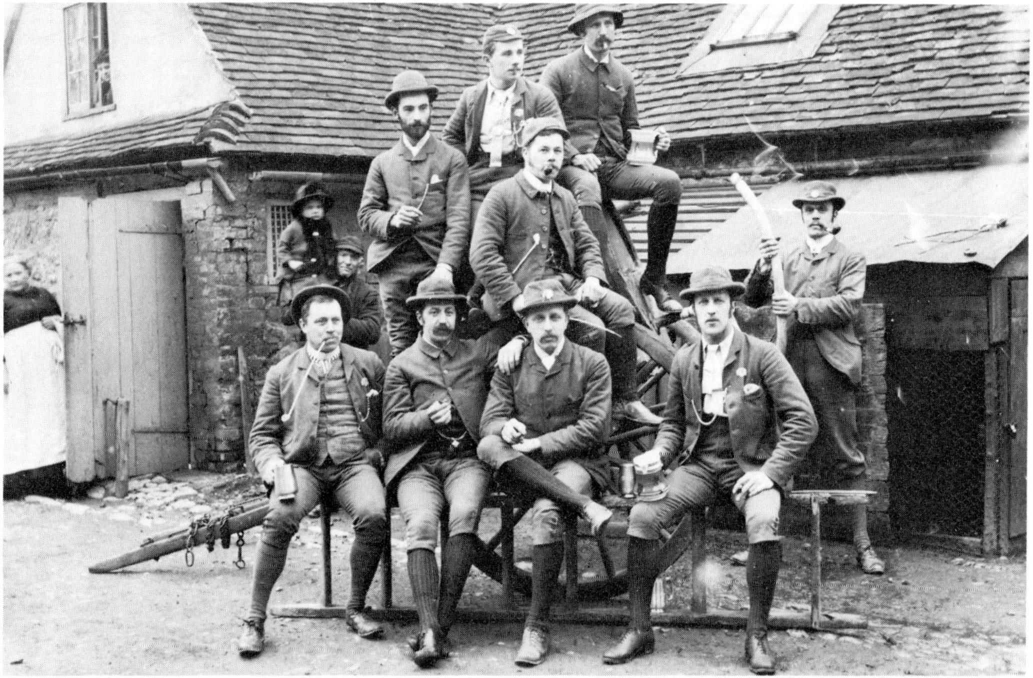

71. Only the glazed tile pilasters with helmeted head and crossed torches, either side of the shop window (see left of previous card) remain to show that this was once the Headquarters of the Tunbridge Wells and District Steam Fire Brigade. Formerly known as the Volunteer Brigade, the name was changed when the old horse-drawn manual was replaced by a Daimler engine. This photograph of about 1890 portrays members of the brigade with one of their horse carts, of which they had three located in different parts of the town. The Volunteer Fire Brigade had been formed in 1866 after a disastrous fire drew attention to the inadequacies of the Borough Fire Brigade (established in 1845). In 1882 Edward Westbrook was appointed Captain of the Borough Brigade with instructions to reorganise it on efficient lines; as the Borough Brigade improved, the Volunteer Brigade became less necessary and was eventually disbanded.

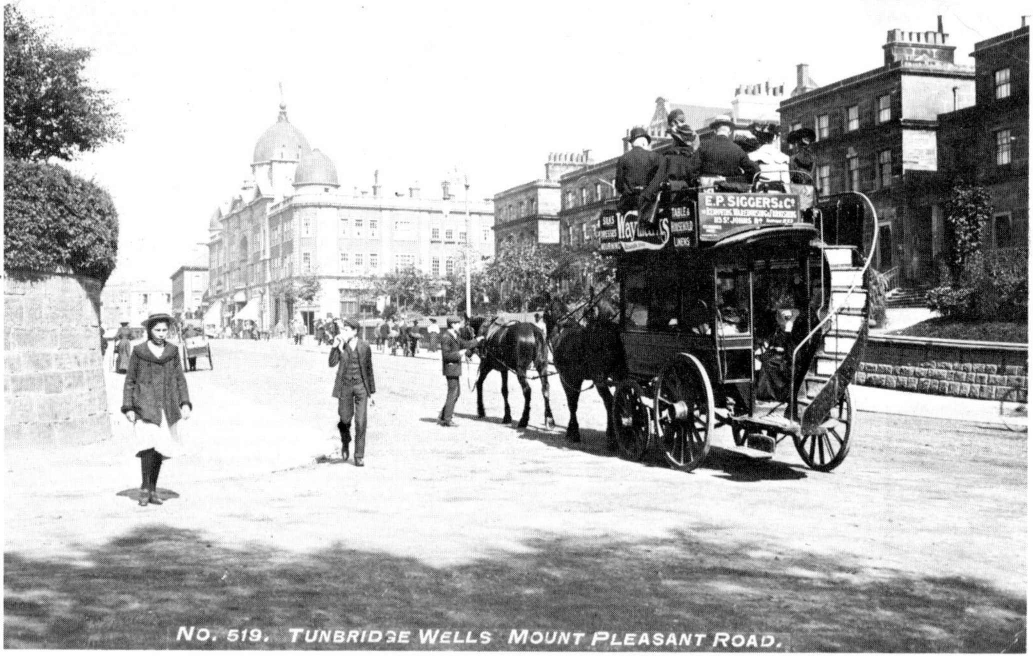

72. Intermittently 'self-propelled buses' had been discussed and briefly tried, but in 1905, the approximate date of this card, the horse bus was the principal means of local transport apart from Bathchairs and hackney carriages. By this date there was only one company operating, the Tunbridge Wells, Southborough and District Omnibus Company Limited, founded in 1896. In response to public complaints over cruelty to horses due to overloading, the Council insisted that a third leading horse should be used on steep hills if more than sixteen passengers were being carried on double-deck buses. Here the Company bus still has the third horse attached after the uphill drag from the Central Railway Station. Despite the failure of earlier attempts at establishing motor bus services, in 1908 the Autocar Company started advertising and within two years had forced the horse bus company into voluntary liquidation.

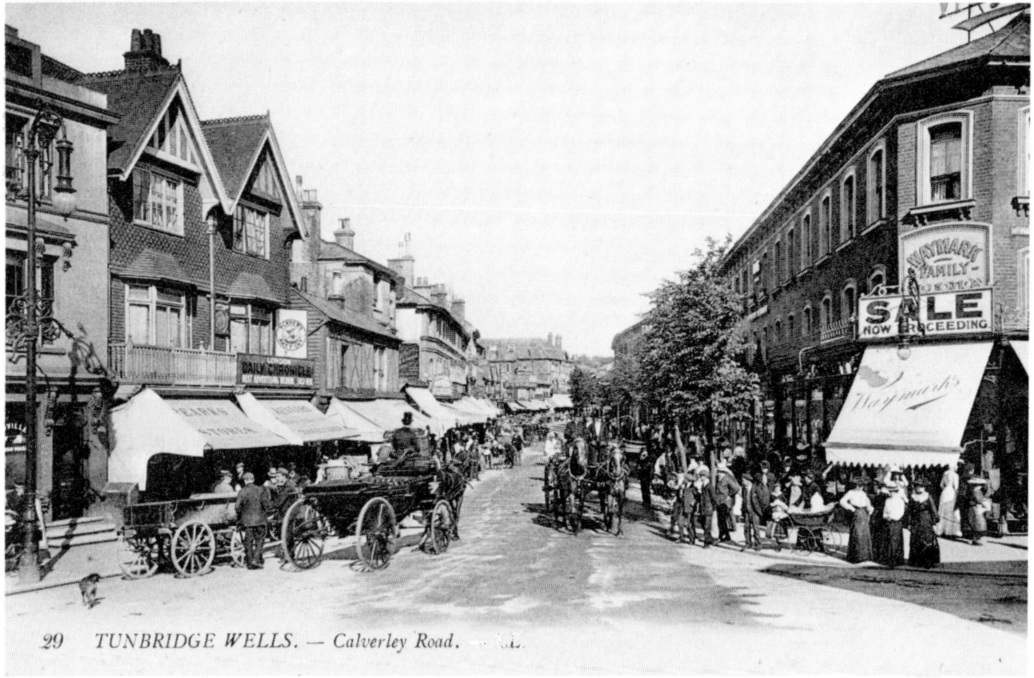

73. Here and there an older building survives among the modern multiple stores on the north side of Calverley Road, once known as Bankrupts Row; but the Grosvenor Tavern on the extreme left and many of the shops beyond the gables (that are still a familiar landmark) have gone. On this side of the street a market was held on Saturday afternoons and evenings in the early years of the century and for some time after the Great War. Regulations were strict, no stallholders being allowed in Calverley Road until the stroke of one, when they poured in from the side streets jostling to secure the best pitches. Children were taken there as a treat to partake of toffee apples made on the spot, or sugar mice, cockles and mussels, jellied eels or whelks. Other barrows vended clothing, china and the like. By late afternoon respectable folk departed leaving the street to the drunks from the nearby public houses.

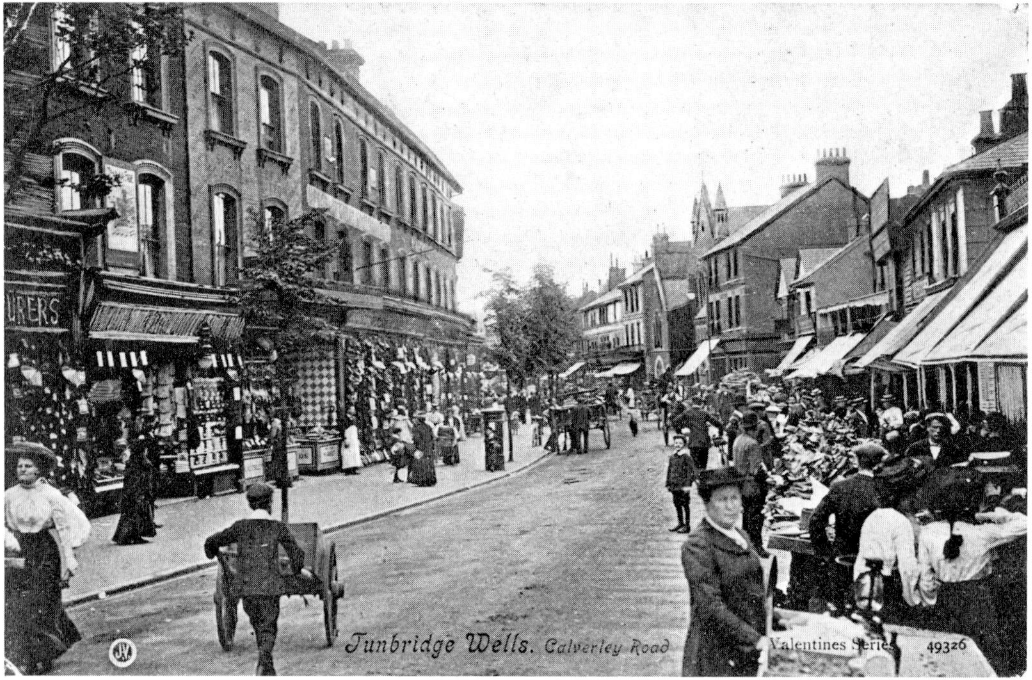

74. The upper façade of the shopping terrace on the south side of Calverley Road, built by Charles Adie in the 1870's, is virtually unchanged since the beginning of the century. Opposite, many of the buildings seen here have disappeared, including the gothic structure of the Baptist Tabernacle, designed by the London architects Lander and Bedells. In 1873 certain members of the Baptist community determined on forming a new Church with an Open Table to all Believers after the Faith and Order of the Metropolitan Tabernacle. Initially services were held in the old Town Hall, but on 1st January 1884 the Tabernacle was opened in what was then the busiest and noisiest street in Tunbridge Wells. In 1928 a 'scheme of re-electrification' made it 'one of the brightest and best lighted of the many places of worship in the Town'. Ten years later the church removed to Upper Grosvenor Road and the Tabernacle was demolished.

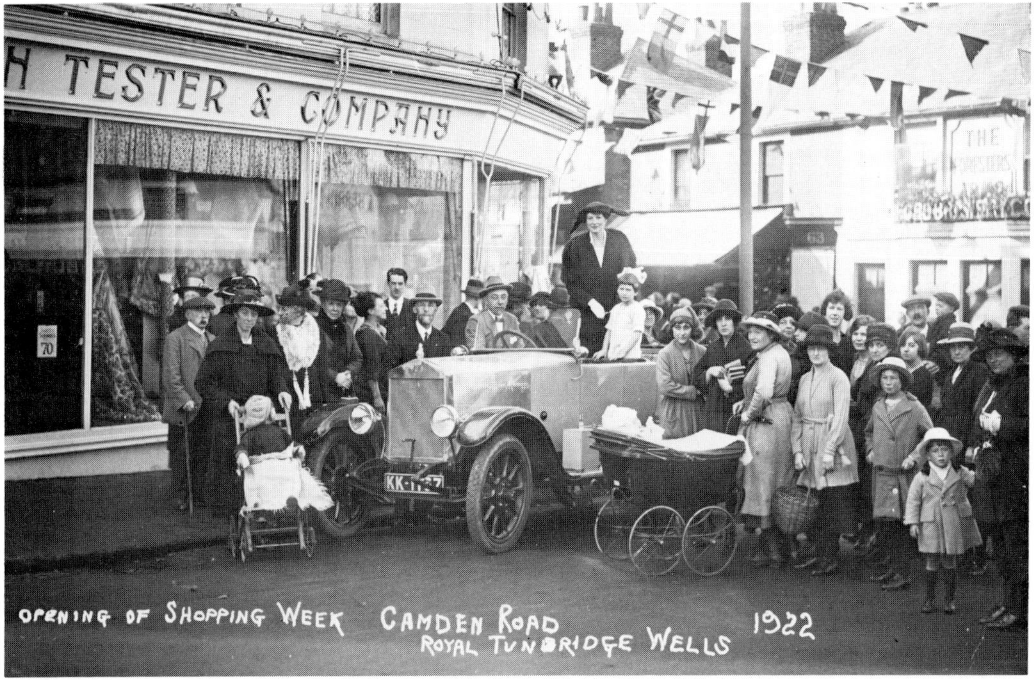

75. Described by many as the greatest publicity campaign ever organised for the benefit of the tradesmen, Tunbridge Wells Shopping Week and Carnival opened simultaneously at seven different points in the town on 16th October 1922. In Camden Road after Alderman C.E. Westbrook's witty opening speech, the wife of Reverend W.J. Torrance released gas-filled balloons, one of which was picked up as far away as Swindon. Because of the wide distribution of advertising booklets with free gift numbers, the main thoroughfares were congested with thousands of people wending their way from shop to shop in expectancy of finding their lucky number against an article displayed in one of the windows. Flags adorned the streets and shop premises were decorated; those of John Tester & Co., general drapers, which extended from No. 42 to No. 54 Camden Road, were brilliantly illuminated by festoons of many coloured electric lights.

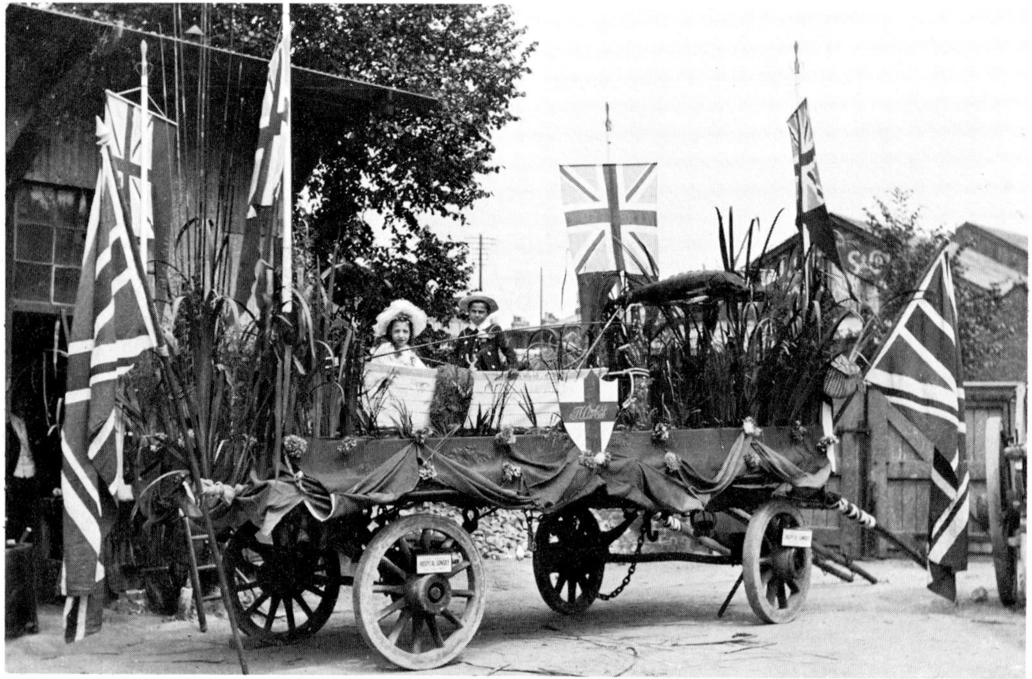

76. Another rare postcard depicts the decorated float of the Angling Society waiting to join the Hospital Sunday Parade organised by the Tunbridge Wells Friendly Society on 21st July 1907. A contemporary account describes how *The procession was formed in Camden Road early in the afternoon and extended for a considerable distance. A body of local police led off, followed by the drum and fife band of the local Volunteer Corps, and the Fire Brigade's Band. Nearly all the Friendly Societies brought a banner of the Order and the decorated cars, especially that of the Angling Society were skilfully done. Huge crowds lined the streets traversed by the processionalists, and the collectors with a persistence worthy of the excellent cause, made every effort to make the total sum realised a record one. After parading the principal thoroughfares... the procession arrived at Mount Pleasant Congregational Church.*

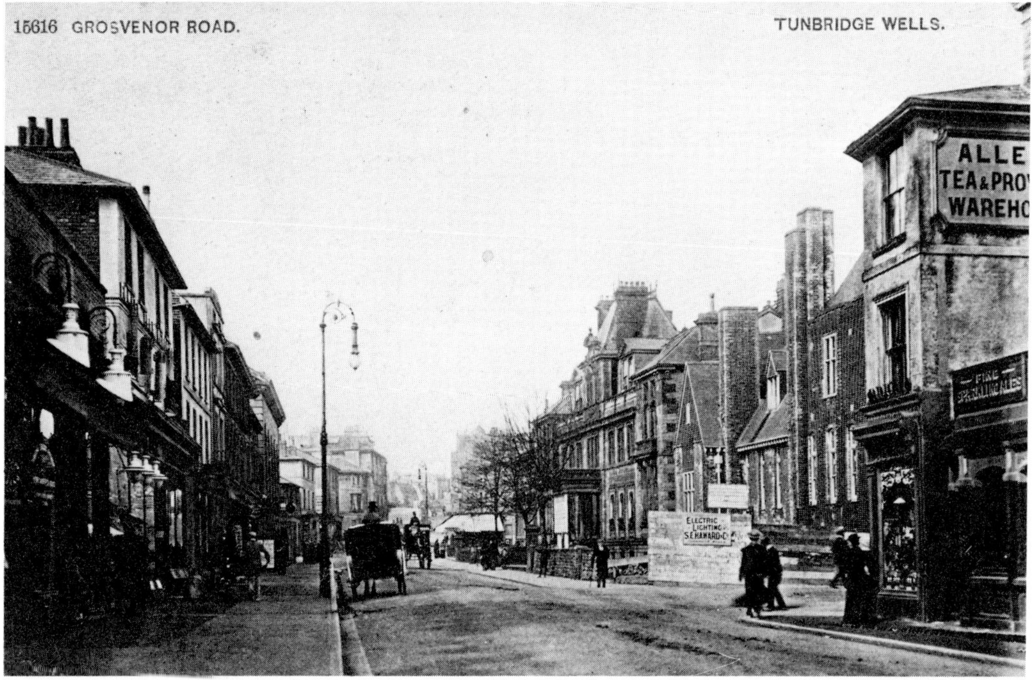

77. The central part of this view of Grosvenor Road taken about 1905 is scarcely recognisable. On the right stands the old General Hospital built in 1842 with new wings completed in 1870, a third storey added in 1884 and a further extension on the corner of Goods Station Road opened in 1904. The name was changed from the original Dispensary and Infirmary to the General Hospital in 1884 as it had tended to be confused with the workhouse infirmary; and on moving to new premises on Mount Ephraim in 1934, it was renamed the Kent and Sussex Hospital. Most of the old buildings were then pulled down to make way for the present Five Ways Post Office and block of shops known as Coronation Parade in honour of the year of their construction (1937). Halfway up the road on the left, at the corner of Hanover Road, is the Roman Catholic Church of St. Augustine, opened July 1838 and demolished in 1968 to be replaced by a supermarket.

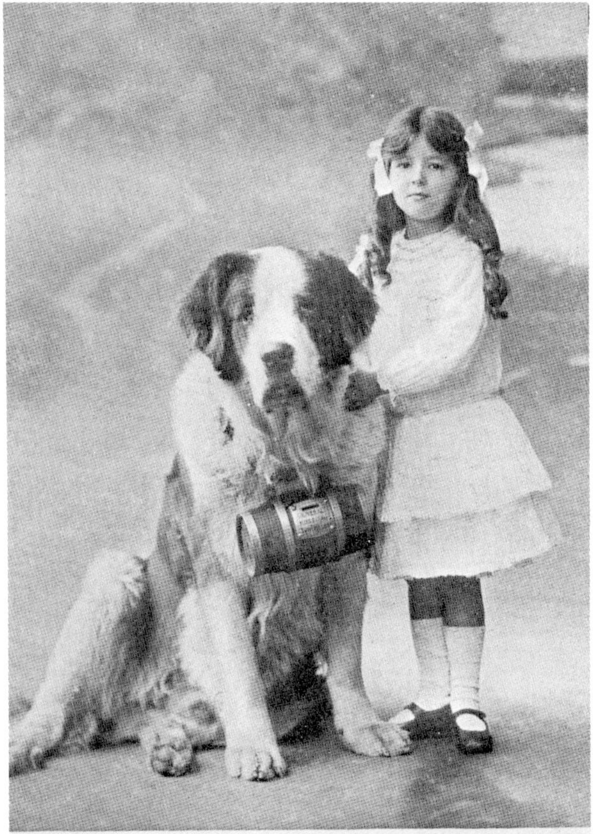

"LEO," Canine Collector for the General Hospital, Tunbridge Wells, and one of his little Friends.

78. Throughout its history, voluntary contributions by way of annual subscriptions, donations and box collections were an important source of income for the General Hospital and initially its only revenue. The original Dispensary had started in 1829 as a charity to assist the sick poor of the town. In the early years contributions exceeded annual expenditure, and when the institution moved to Grosvenor Road, the Trustees were able to invest a substantial surplus from the building funds; but as the hospital commitments and expenses increased, new forms of fund raising had to be found. In the 1880's Tunbridge Wells Hospital Saturday and Sunday Funds were inaugurated and an ingenious Mr. W. Skinner collected from the 'Very Poor'. For some years at the beginning of this century, the St. Bernard dog Leo, owned by the Matron of Mount Ephraim Nursing Home, carried a barrel-shaped collecting box in aid of the Hospital.

79. For over twenty years W. Skinner collected from the 'Very Poor' in aid of the General Hospital, on the principle that 'Many a mickle makes a muckle'. His may have been the inspiration for R. Arnold's collection of farthings for the charity that provided breakfasts for London slum children. Significantly he shared the same address in Mount Pleasant as the photographer Percy S. Lankester (and incidentally, the Young Men's Christian Association). As well as producing photographs for illustrated guide books, children's portraiture and grand portraits of notabilities, Lankester seems to have prided himself on being on the spot to record the unusual. Many of his pictures appear in local newspapers and some he reproduced as postcards (Nos. 1, 8, 9, 15 and 52). The idea for this unusual photograph was probably Lankester's, proceeds from the postcard sales being his contribution to his neighbour's favourite charity.

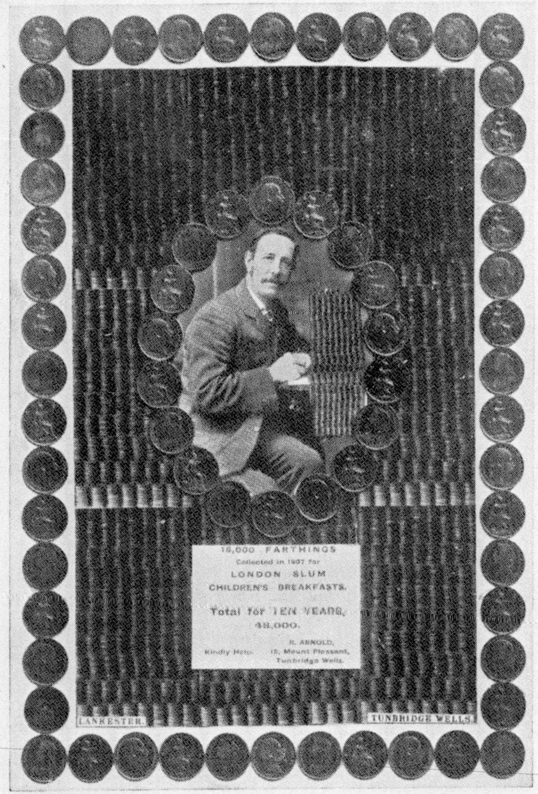

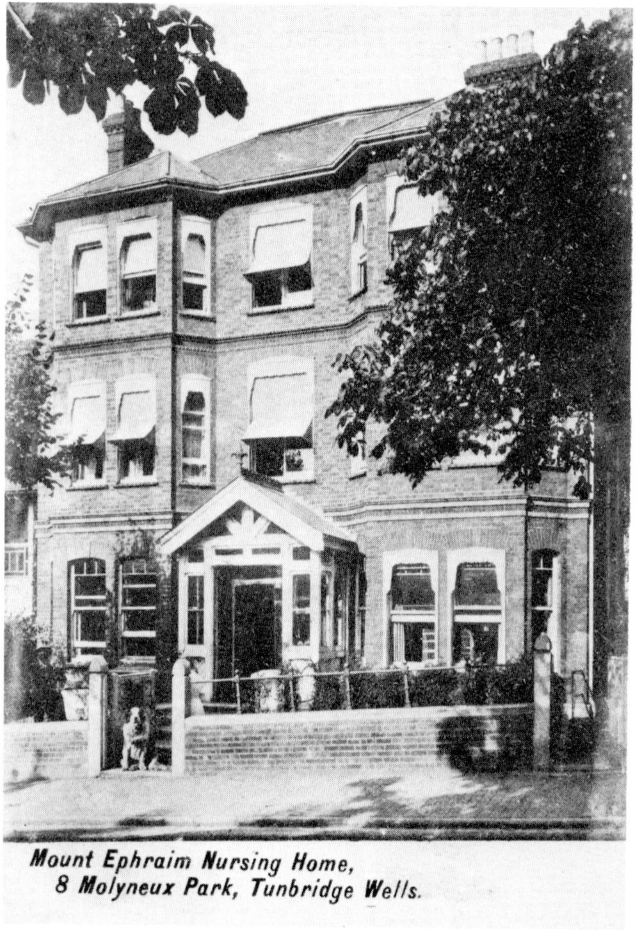

80. The Mount Ephraim Nursing Home in Molyneux Park was run by Miss Baxter, a former superintendent of the County and City of York Hospital. Owner of the famous canine collector for the General Hospital (seated at gate), she adopted his name for the telegraphic address of her establishment, 'Leo, Tunbridge Wells'. The nursing home was advertised as receiving 'medical, surgical, Weir-Mitchell and accouchement cases', providing 'dowsing, radiant-light and heat baths, Swedish massage, etc.', and able to supply trained nurses and masseuses for private cases. Soon after this picture was taken in about 1905, the gabled porch was replaced with a glazed entrance supporting a balcony, with access from the house through a French window; later there were sun balconies on each floor. In the 1930's the nursing home became Barons Court Hotel, which still exists.

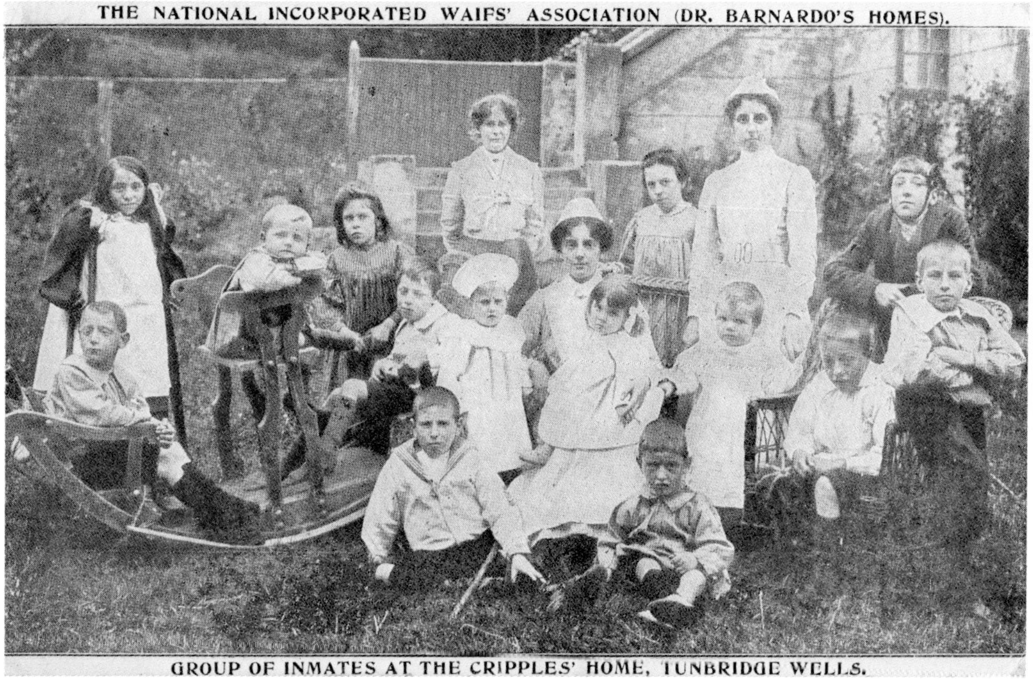

81. Some of the forty-five children cared for at Dr. Barnardo's home are photographed here in the grounds of Agra House, 19 Park Road about 1907. At that time it took £16 a year to train an ordinary child and £30 to rear a sick or crippled child. A contemporary commented: 'Not, perhaps, without good reason did the great pioneer pick Tunbridge Wells, where so many wealthy reside, as the place to locate a home for little incurables, a home for crippled children.' All the money required for the purchase of Agra House (£2,500) was raised locally and on 18th December 1902 it was opened as a hospital home for crippled and invalid children. In 1936 it was decided to look for an alternative site for the erection of new buildings, as a result of which Ormonde Lodge, Southborough was bought in 1938, the old house demolished and Meadow School built. In March 1939 Agra House itself was sold by auction and later demolished. Park Court now occupies the site.

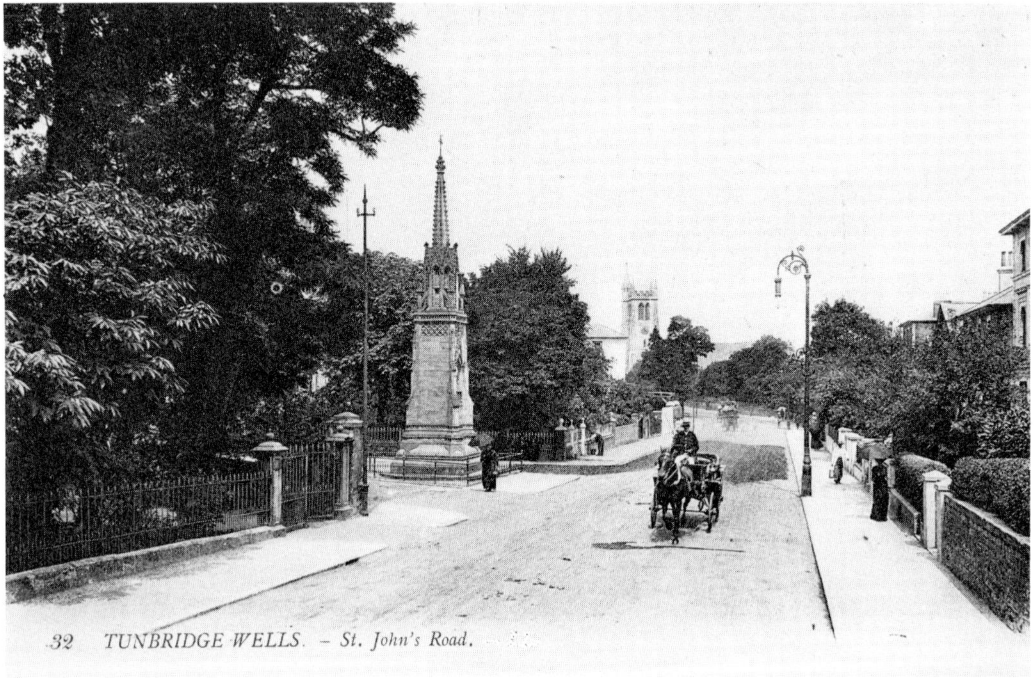

82. When Canon Edward Hoare, 'the Protestant Pontiff of Tunbridge Wells', died in 1894 at the age of eighty-seven, blind but still active in his capacity as Vicar of Holy Trinity, the whole town grieved. For some forty years he had dominated the religious life of the community, filling the church to overflowing. It was even said that people came to live in Tunbridge Wells in order to hear his sermons. The gothic memorial with portrait plaque by John Oldrid was erected at the entrance to Culverden Park Road in Jubilee Year; in 1980 it was threatened with demolition as part of a road widening scheme. In the event, it proved possible to shift bodily the complete monument a few yards to one side. The gardens and houses that lay behind on the left of St. John's Road have all been swept away; the Automatic Telephone Exchange Trunk Switching Centre and Repeater Station, opened in 1965, occupies the site in the foreground of this Edwardian card.

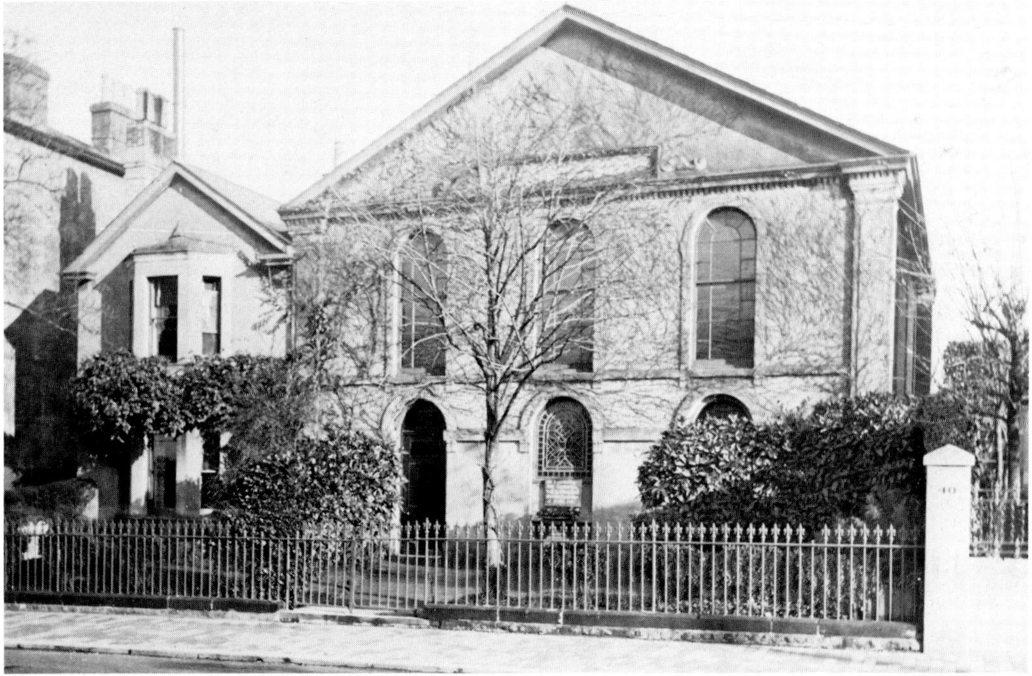

83. On the site in St. John's Road, now occupied by the Maidstone and District Motor Services Depot, formerly stood the non-conformist Salem Chapel, built in 1866 by Thomas Edwards author of the hymn book 'Waters in the Wilderness'. Living in the adjoining cottage, he preached there for twenty-seven years and drew large crowds to services held on the Common on Sunday afternoons. When James Mountain resigned from the pastorate of Emmanuel Church in 1897 on the grounds that he no longer agreed with infant baptism (see No. 45), he was persuaded by many of his congregation to remain in Tunbridge Wells. For a couple of years until new premises could be built, he and his followers occupied Salem Chapel, temporarily changing its name to St. John's Road Free Church. In 1935 the chapel was purchased by the bus company, and once the adjacent property had been acquired all the buildings were demolished to make way for the present garage.

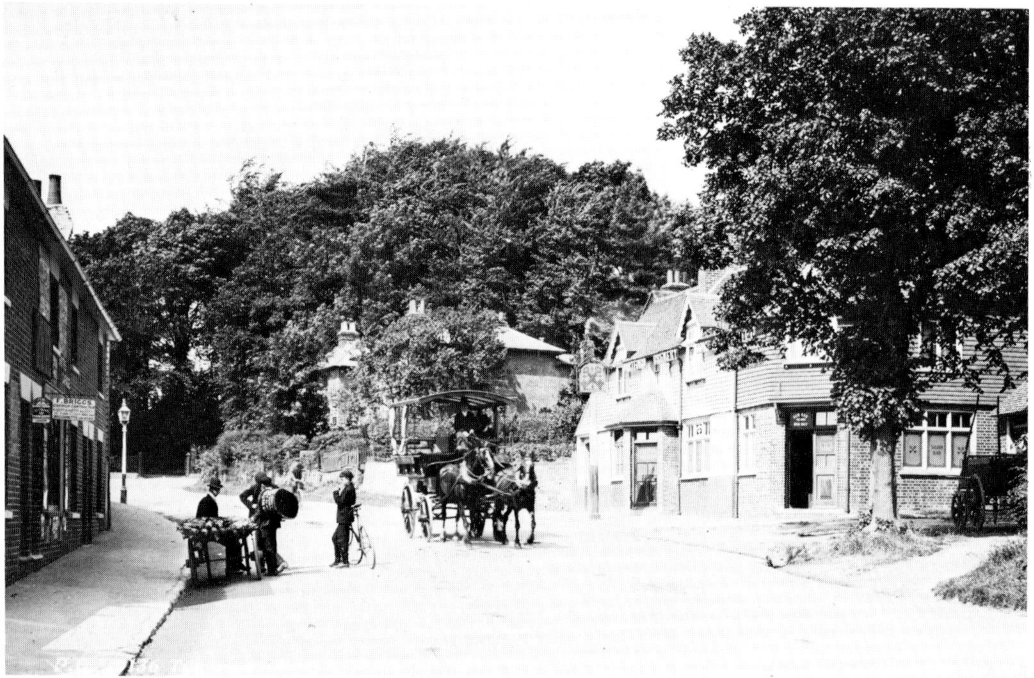

84. When this Edwardian view of St. John's Road at the Powder Mill Lane junction was taken, the Cross Keys was supplied by the Dartford Brewery Co. Ltd. of Tonbridge. Of the row of cottages beyond on the site of the public house car park, the nearest was demolished by gales in 1925 (see next postcard), its neighbour pulled down in the early thirties having probably become structurally unsafe, and the remaining four removed just before the Second World War. On the other side, the terrace houses were demolished in the 1950's, their site now forming part of the Boys' Grammar School grounds. Outside the general shop of Frederick Briggs, who occupied the premises for some twenty years at the beginning of the century, the fishmonger's barrow is attended by various errand boys, one of them with a carrying box from William Waters, the draper's shop in Camden Road.

85. Gales which swept the whole country demolished a house near the corner of Powder Mill Lane and St. John's Road at the beginning of January 1925. *The first damage was done on Tuesday afternoon, when the South side of the house gave way, thus loosening the joists and rendering the adjoining bedroom and staircase unsafe for use. In spite of the continuation of the gale, and the fact that the house was doomed to destruction, the occupants remained in possession and reached the bedrooms, which remained sound, by means of a ladder... The house finally collapsed at 10.15 on Friday night. Although the house was very old, the foundation and general structure may have been weakened by the digging of a cellar, which was hewn out of solid rock, some time after the erection of the cottage, which was one of a semi-detached pair. The remaining habitation (now detached) is still tenanted, and appears to be quite sound.*

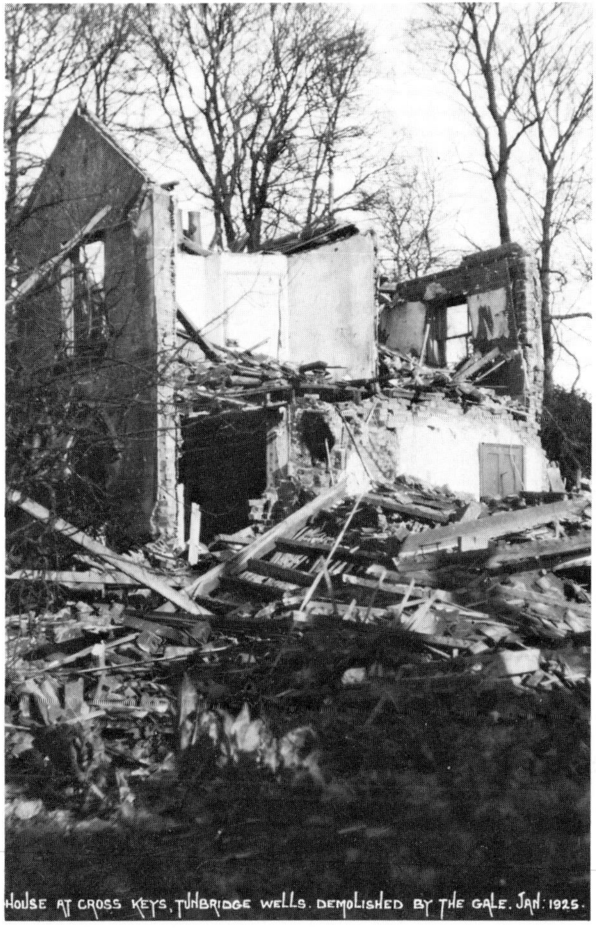

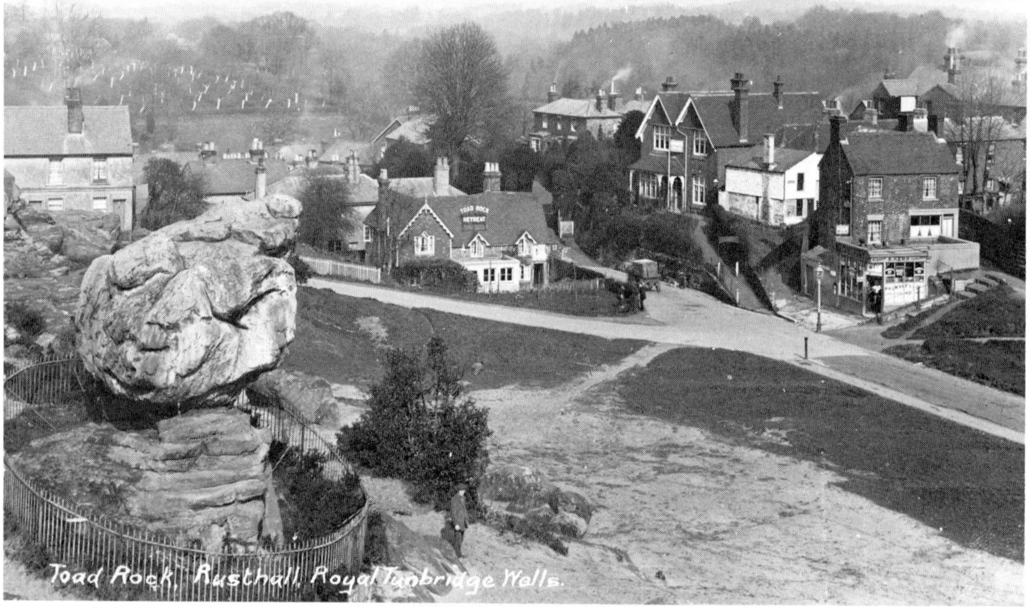

86. *Having reached Rusthall Common, the visitor may turn to the right by a path which conducts to a small verdant amphitheatre, the central figure wherein is a colossal stone, which has long been known as the Toad Rock, and is considered one of the 'sights' of Tunbridge Wells. The resemblance of this mass of sandstone to an immense toad is certainly striking.* This postcard of Toad Rock was published about 1913 by Agnes Kemp of The Stores, Denny Bottom, whose grocer's shop appears to the right of the photograph. The store survives but the white cottage behind has since been pulled down; and the orchards beyond the Toad Rock Retreat were uprooted in the early thirties to provide building land for the Grange Road estate. Whitened trunks and lower branches used to be a familiar sight in Kentish orchards, when fruit growers painted them with limewash to eradicate the lichen that harboured overwintering pests and their eggs.

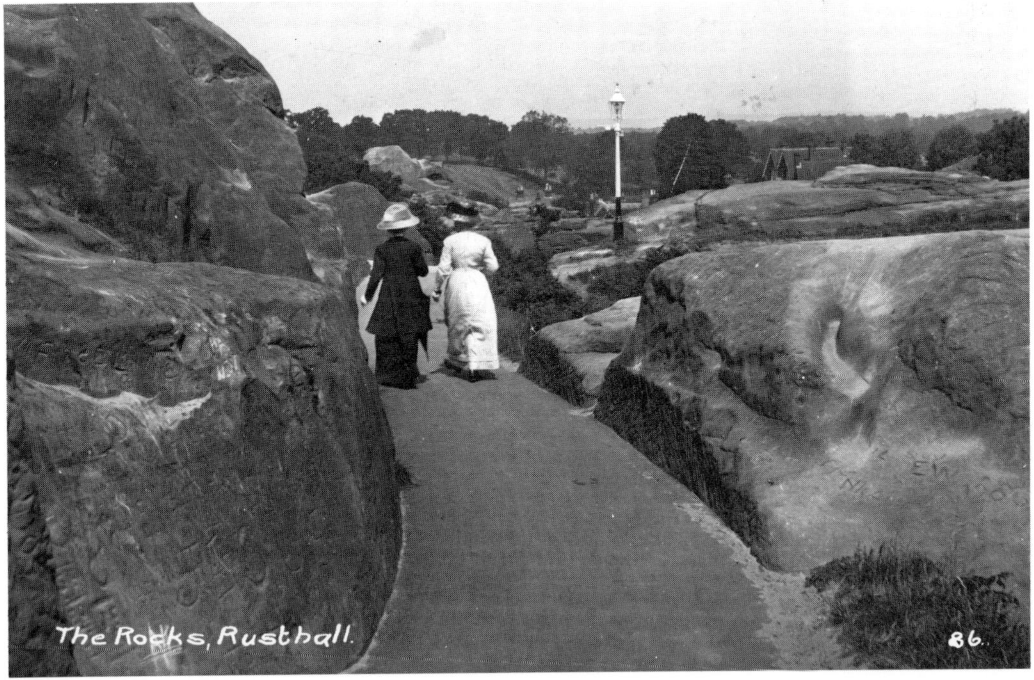

87. *The great feature of interest attaching to Rusthall Common is of course, the Toad Rock and its craggy surroundings... When as a visitor you explore this locality, you will soon discover that you are an object of mercenary interest, and almost before you are aware of it you are under the guidance of a self-appointed cicerone, and from his lips will learn that well nigh every rock has its name derived from a fancied resemblance to the things mentioned. A very strong fancy is required in most cases. But if 'you make believe hard enough' you can almost see a resemblance between the rock which you are told is the Pulpit Rock and a pulpit; and the same may apply to the Little Toad, the Elephant, the Fox's Hole, the Footsteps, the Cottage Loaf, the Parson's Face, the Cradle, the Bloodstain, the Lion and the Pig's Head Rocks, and we believe there are a few score more.*

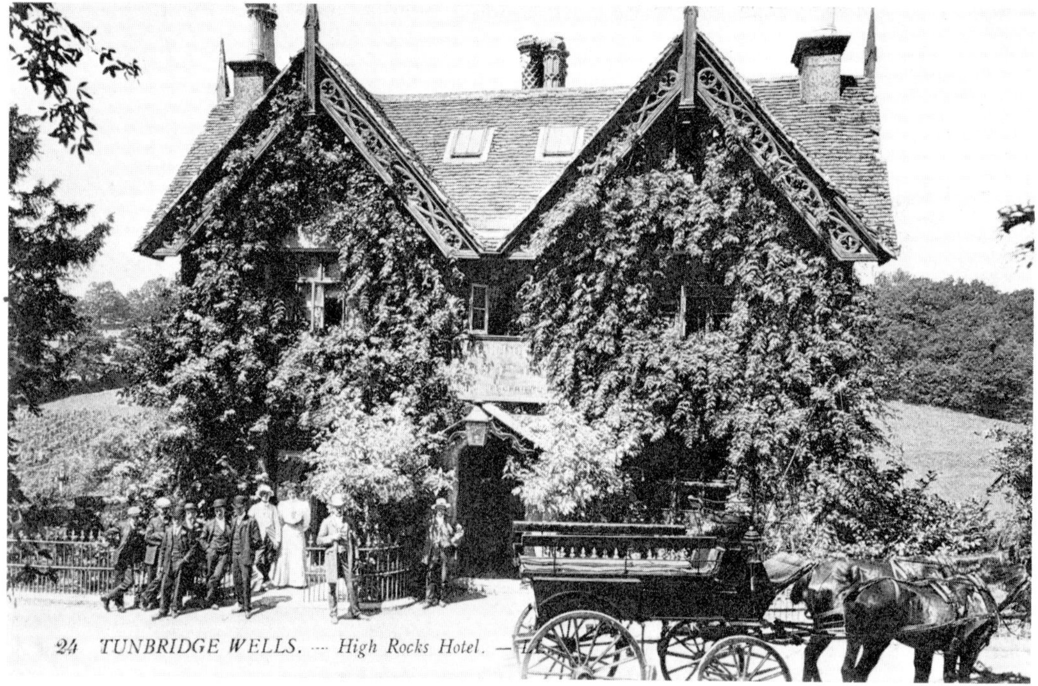

88. *No visitor to Tunbridge Wells is likely to leave without taking an opportunity of seeing the High Rocks, that wonderful assemblage of masses of sandstone – since this is one of the 'lions' of the place. These rocks are situated about a mile-and-a-half from the Pantiles in a south-westerly direction, and can be approached via the Common, Hungershall Park, and High Rocks Lane. In front of the entrance to the grounds in which the rocks stand, is an inn with the particularly inappropriate name of 'The Cape of Good Hope'* – so wrote the author of a pictorial history of Tunbridge Wells in 1892. Writers of earlier guides found the appellation 'cheering' and commented on the 'refreshing words under it – Fine Bottled Beer, Porter, Cider, Soda Water, Spruce and Ginger Beer, Tea, Coffee, Rock Cakes, &c.' By the end of the century the old seventeenth century hostelry had been renamed the High Rocks Hotel, and is now known as the High Rocks Inn.

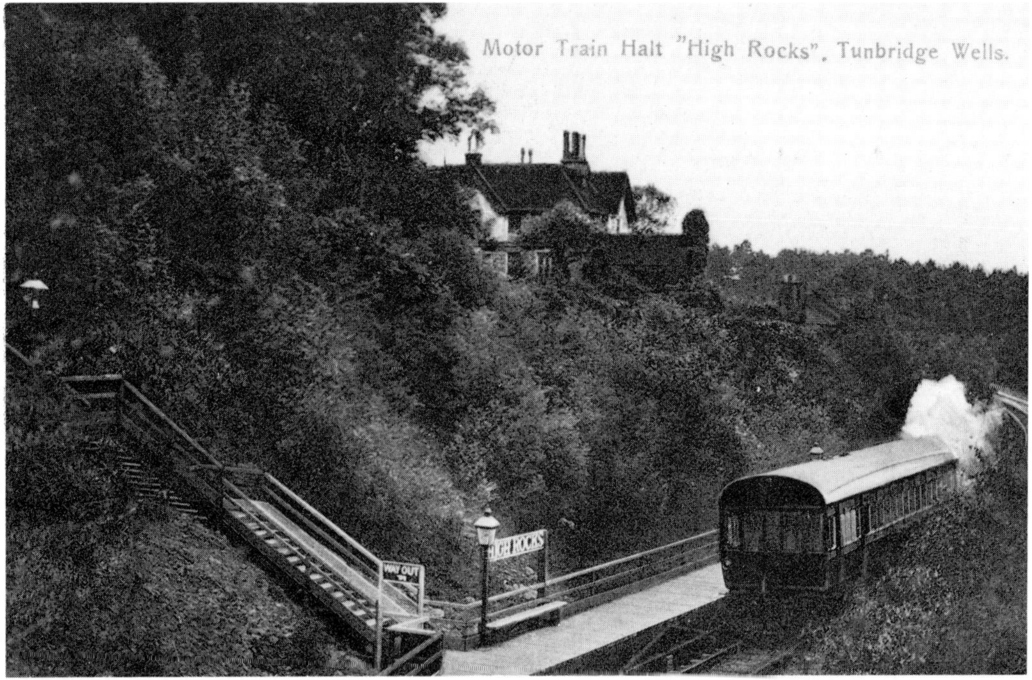

89. A visit to High Rocks and Broadwater Forest was one of the morning walks around the town recommended by Victorian and Edwardian guide books. For the less energetic, open passenger carts were available, a service provided at one time by James F. White, the licensee of the High Rocks and Cape of Good Hope Hotel. His horse-drawn breaks ran at intervals from the stand in London Road to the entrance of High Rocks, for a fare of sixpence each way. At one time it was also possible to arrive by train, alighting at High Rocks Halt, the first station out from Tunbridge Wells on the Brighton line. The landlord of the hotel rented the grounds containing the famous rocks, to which he charged a sixpence admission fee. As well as the natural features to be explored and wondered at, amusements of various kinds were provided including swings and see-saws for the children, and in winter skating on the Trout Lake when frozen.

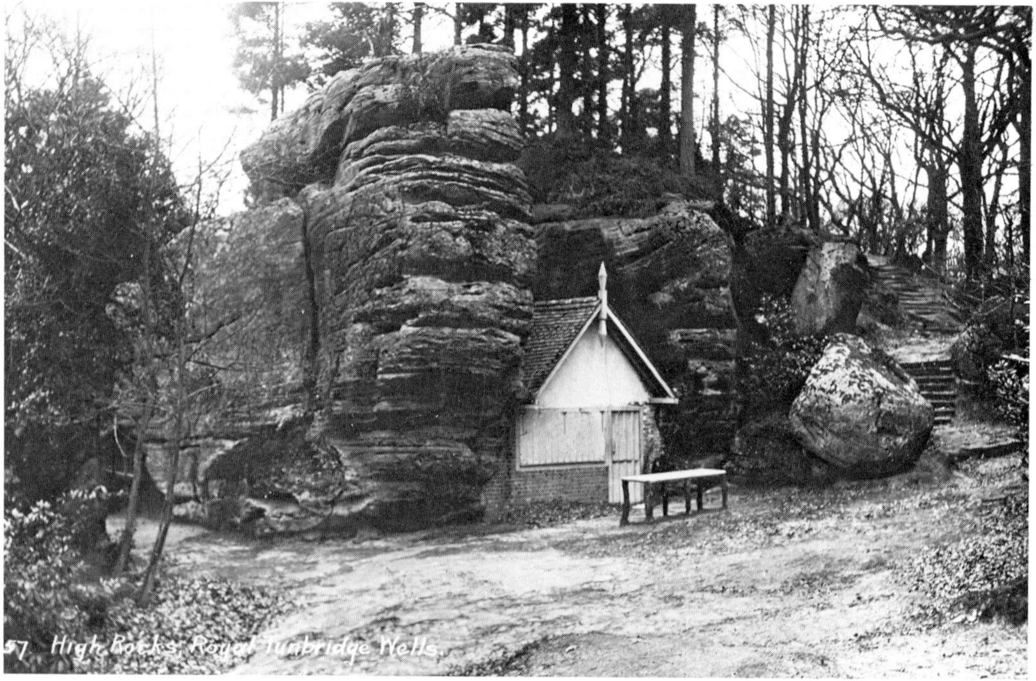

90. In the eighteenth and nineteenth centuries there were several small tea-houses and summer-houses where visitors might partake of refreshments; some have completely vanished, of others only the foundations survive. This tea-house wedged between two rocky outcrops, on a postcard dated 1915, is recognisable in early Victorian engravings and its delapidated shell survived until quite recently. After the Second World War when High Rocks again experienced a period of neglect, the old tea-house was renovated and converted into the Alpine Hut of the Sandstone Climbing Club of Great Britain, who for some years had their headquarters there and held training sessions on the rocks.

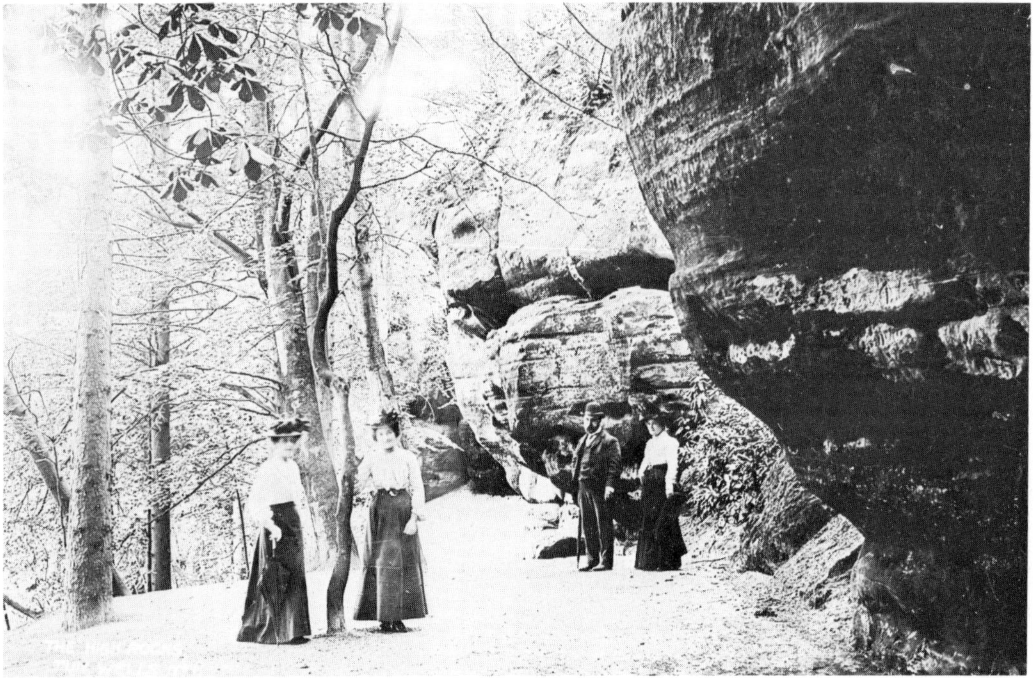

91. Almost as popular as those of the Pantiles and the Common, were Edwardian postcards of High Rocks, particularly those illustrating the wooden bridge across the main chasm. Rarer is this view taken near the entrance to the Bell Rock, *so called because it yields a metallic ring when struck, as it pretty often is, with the mighty cudgels which lie ready to hand. It is most creditable to this much-belaboured and bedinted mass that it still survives its cruel fate! The rock is sacred to the memory of a lap-dog which met with an untimely end by falling down into this narrow fissure. Here is the epitaph: a guide-book writer was heartless enough to term it dog-gerel! '1702 / This scratch I make that you may know / On this rock lyes the beauteous Bow; / Reader, this Rock is the Bow's Bell, / Strike't with thy stick and ring his knell.'* From other authors' comments it would appear that to hear the metallic ring required ears of imagination.

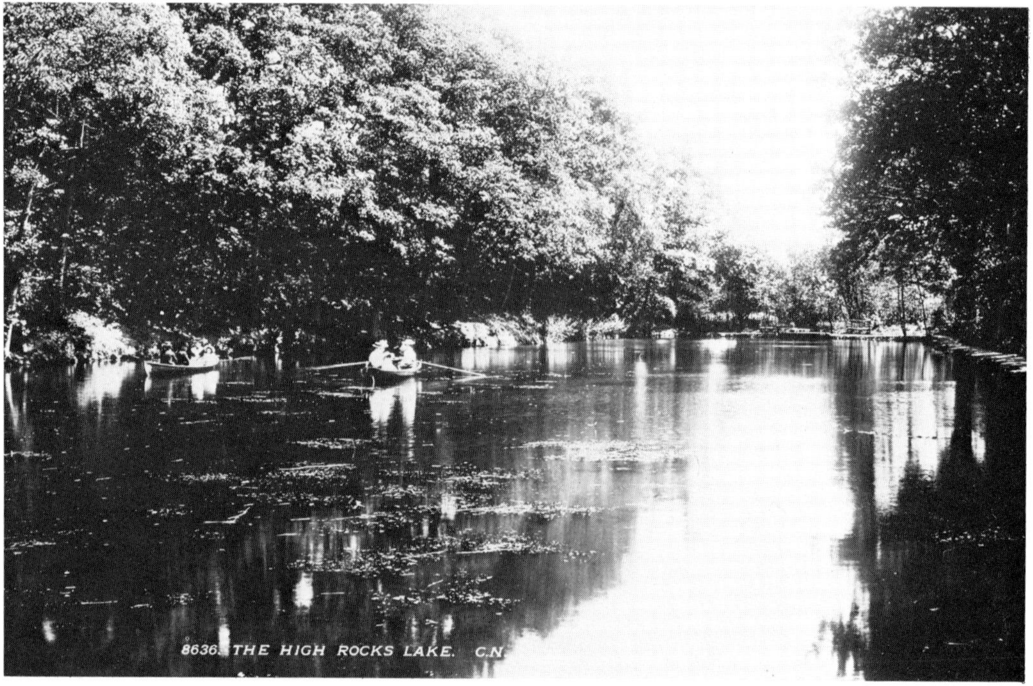

92. *Having passed out of the Rock grounds proper, we turn left and enter the gate that leads to the lake. Passing the little winding way between verdant bowers of rhododendron, we descend to the margin of the pretty sheltered sheet of water. There are enough aquatic plants in the lake to make it at all times picturesque. The water lily, great reed mace, and water plantain are thriving... It is a spot where one may dream and muse, and whether we cross the bridge and sit upon the island, or lounge in the many nooks upon the margin of the lake, or take our turn in the splendid boats, there is a peacefulness and restfulness that will entrance both old and young alike.* Popular at the beginning of the century, over the years the lake fell into neglect and deteriorated to little more than a marsh. Although the present proprietor has dredged the lake, it is unlikely that it will ever again sport rowing boats for lazy summer afternoons.